The Bitch, The Crone

and

The Harlot

Reclaiming the Magical Feminine in Midlife

Susan Schachterle

www.BitchCroneHarlot.com

Elite Books

Santa Rosa, CA 95403

www.EliteBooksOnline.com

Library of Congress Cataloging-in-Publication Data

Schachterle, Susan.

The Bitch, the Crone, and the Harlot: reclaiming the magical feminine in midlife / Susan Schachterle.

p. cm.

Includes bibliographic references.

ISBN-13: 978-1-60070-028-6 (hardcover)
ISBN-10: 1-60070-028-4 (hardcover)
ISBN-13: 978-1-60070-018-7 (softcover)
ISBN-10: 1-60070-018-7 (softcover)

1. Middle-aged women—Conduct of life. 2. Middle-aged women—Psychology. 3. Self-actualization in women. 4. Archetype (Psychology) I. Title.

HQ1059.4.S365 2006

155.3'33—dc22

2006031839

Cover design by Richard Martin, RichImage.com © 2006

Author photograph by Susan Godard

Copyediting by Courtney Arnold

Typesetting by Karin Kinsey

Typeset in Hoefler Text

Printed in USA by Sheridan Books, www.SheridanBooks.com

First Edition

10 9 8 7 6 5 4 3 2 1

Acknowledgments

I am grateful to Dawson Church and the lovely and talented people at Elite Books for their guidance and assistance as I gave birth to *The Bitch, The Crone, and The Harlot* ... not necessarily an easy birth, but much more peaceful and passionate with them as midwives.

And I dedicate this labor of love to those I cherish more than anything in life:

To my children, the lights of my life, and the many lessons in love, patience, and trust they have taught me;

To my father, for the capacity for discipline and commitment he has passed on to me;

To my mother, for the faith she has shared; and, ultimately and eternally, to Spirit, whose, love, patience, wisdom, and power continue to amaze me.

Contents

YOU·WE·RE·BORN·complete

...EVERYTHING YOU NEED TO BE AN extraordinary individual, YOU CARRIED WITH YOU INTO LIFE!

...AT every moment I HAVE THE OPPORTUNITY FOR J·O·Y!

Introduction

You were born complete. Everything you need to be an extraordinary individual and to live in an extraordinary way, you carried with you into life. I remember so well the moment at which I first began to grasp this. A man I had loved wildly had suddenly, and in a painful way, left me. Creativity, humor, elegance, and passion had shaped our five-year-long relationship, and I grieved deeply for months, mourning the fact that I would never again be creative, humorous, elegant, or passionate. After all, I reasoned, this man had been the source of those things between us; I had simply tagged along, enjoying the fruits of his exceptional essence. I found myself feeling dowdy, boring, and superficial without him to open the door to that way of being I had come to appreciate.

One day, at about the six-month point in my sorrow and feeling stuck in an overwhelming despair, I raged toward heaven, accusing Spirit of snatching from me the only source of joy I would ever have. "How could you do this to me?" I whined; "How could you give me a glimpse of all those wonderful things and then take them away? You are a cruel and thoughtless God." Suddenly, in a blinding flash, I understood. My lover had not been the source of everything that had made the relationship remarkable; he had been a catalyst for my finding those things within myself. He was a unique and outstanding man, and I had loved him deeply. However, he had not created the power, passion, and vibrancy had felt with him; he had only helped to bring to the surface qualities and capacities that were part of me, but which I hadn't been aware of. This realization changed my outlook almost immediately. Although I still missed him, I now understood that I carried in me the ability to experience all the things I had loved about the relationship. That meant that at every moment, even all by myself, I had the opportunity for joy.

This was an important thing for me to remember, especially as I approached midlife. It was at that point that I found myself faced with a choice: How would I choose to enter this next part of my life? I could regard it as an indication that the end was near—that I no longer had value and should make room for younger women who were more significant than myself. Or I could recognize the potential inherent in this stage of life, and with dignity and delight, move deeper into the power, wisdom, and sensuality that had always been part of me. It was up to me, and the choice I made would have a profound impact on the rest of my life.

In the minds of many, midlife signals the beginning of the end, that final stretch of road leading directly and relentlessly toward death. The result of this perspective is often either a desperate and sometimes embarrassing attempt to cling to youth, or an *I'm-powerless-in-the-face-of-aging* resignation that results in going through the motions, existing instead of living. Because society places such emphasis on youth, beauty, and sexuality, anyone approaching midlife still looking for validation from external sources is heading for a fall. Women are especially vulnerable, since more often than not, as young girls, we learn the importance of being cute, just delicate enough to need occasional help, and as sexy as possible. This is the formula that almost guarantees a secure future. Or so we've been told. It can all begin to crumble, however, when those qualities that characterized us during the first half of life no longer fit. As we metamorphose into beings whose value lies deeper, we must be willing to change the formula.

The archetypes that shape women's early choices become obvious when we are children, and may include the Good Girl, the Bright Student, the Seductress, and later the Good Wife and the Nurturing Mother. Each of these has elements that teach us well, and some elements we will struggle to break free from, like a snake shedding a skin it has outgrown. But the positive archetypes appropriate to midlife seem more difficult to find. I've seen the Exhausted and Resentful Old Broad, the Woman Who Gave Up Long Ago, and the Worn Out Old Lady Who Figures She No Longer Matters, but none of these bring passion, possibility, or joy.

In the face of this somewhat hopeless perspective, I propose three very different models for a midlife that brings comprehensive expression of the power, wisdom, and sensuality inherent in the feminine:

The Bitch—a woman who makes things happen without doing damage.

The Crone—a woman who has constant access to a depth of practical wisdom younger women haven't had time to develop.

The Harlot—a woman whose sensuality is used not to manipulate, but rather to express her profound connection to all of life and its Source, and who has also had the time to develop and refine erotic moves younger women have yet to learn.

Each of these uncommon beings lives from an aspect of the feminine that is often left either undeveloped, or underdeveloped. Though living examples of these archetypes may be rare, a deeper exploration reveals that all three are available to each of us.

June 2006

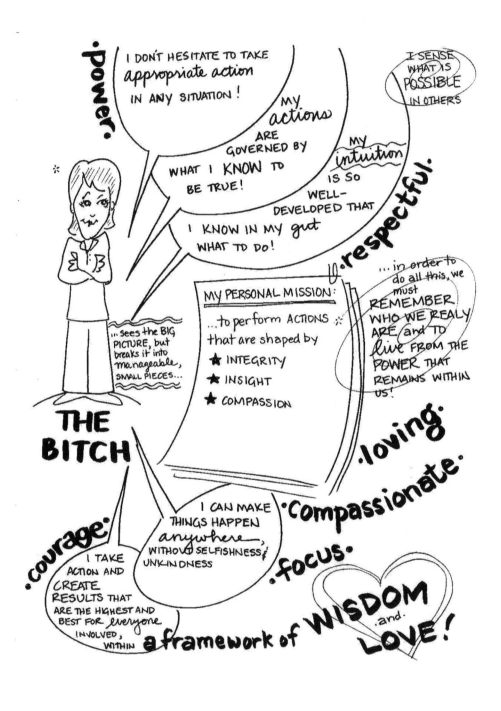

The Bitch:
Power and Possibility

Men and women are different. You may have noticed this. We are necessary compliments to each other in a variety of ways, and we are different. This has nothing to do with equal rights, equal pay, or any of the other arguments for equality that, for the most part, are unwaveringly valid. This has to do with the fact that, unfortunate socialization of gender roles aside, our brains and our psychological and emotional wiring are different so that we can function in different ways and together, ideally at least, bring a comprehensive and complete perspective into our experiences. You have most likely also noticed the more obvious differences between the genders. But the internal differences, those less evident than genitalia and chest hair, are the ones that can enhance or frustrate our attempts to connect. When we choose to understand the way life looks, sounds, and feels from the position of someone different than ourselves, we are in a position to learn, teach, offer options, and in general flow together in a way that is whole. When we choose, instead, to label that different way of perceiving and interpreting things as "wrong," we immediately narrow our own range of possibilities.

A friend once told me that she had come to regard the first half of life as exploration. "It's when you experiment with things and people," she explained, as we met to observe her fiftieth birthday. "You try on political and spiritual ideas to see which ones fit. You may move from relationship to relationship looking for your emotional home. You might try out several careers, hoping to find that perfect way to express who you are. The trouble is that so often, during your first forty or fifty years, you don't know who you are; you're still taking shape." I think she's right. We spend the first half of life shaping our identities like we might put together a jigsaw puzzle, collecting information that fills in the gaps and helps us form the bigger picture of our true and unique nature.

There are several areas in which the perspectives of men and women differ wildly, one of the most obvious being power. We understand it differently, we use it differently, and our expression of it is worlds apart. Men tend to focus on information and action, and their perception of power reflects that focus. With that frame of reference in place, the inclination is to gather enough information to figure out what action to take in order to win at something, fix something, move forward toward something, or otherwise make something happen. At the risk of oversimplifying, it is in making something happen that the goal is met. Men's focus is on *information* and *action*.

Women, on the other hand, are most concerned with connection and relationship, and our power lies within that arena. It is in connecting with others and forming meaningful bonds that we demonstrate power; and it is through those relationships that we are able to make things happen and become an undeniable force in the world. However, a woman who has never learned how to best direct that power can quickly run amok, to all of our detriment.

Several years ago I was leading a discussion about relationships with a group of men ranging in age from twenty-three to eighty-one. In the course of the conversation I asked the group to define "bitch". One of the younger men responded that when he called someone a bitch it meant "woman who won't do what I want her to do". There were nodding heads and murmurs of agreement among the group's members. Then a quiet voice broke through from the back of the room. It was the oldest man in the workshop. "To me," he said softly, "'bitch' means 'woman who gets in a revolving door behind me, and somehow gets out ahead of me.'" There was a stunned silence in the room. This stooped old man, in the midst of a group of self-proclaimed studs, had put a whole new face (and a whole new set of possibilities) on a term that had only been used to belittle and denigrate. The room was quiet for several minutes as the men considered what had been said. The rest of the discussion took a very different tone.

The commonly accepted definition of "bitch" has, intentionally or not, tied women's hands by reinforcing the idea that there are two options possible: Bitch, defined as mean, selfish, harsh, unkind, unattractive, and unacceptable; or Good Girl, defined as lovable, obedient, eager to please, and acceptable. With those as the only choices for defining who we are, we are put in a position from which stepping beyond what's considered appropriate for a woman is dangerous. This becomes even more frustrating at midlife, at which point, if we continue to live as Good Girls, we become invisible and get rolled over by those who consider us a quiet and well-behaved part of the backdrop to life. If we choose to look for respect by being demanding and inflexible, we are regarded as pissy older women who must be placated but not taken seriously. Neither of these characterizations is acceptable, and so a new definition is required. For our purposes, a Bitch at midlife is a woman who has become so comfortable with and respectful of who she is that she doesn't hesitate to take appropriate action in any situation. Her actions are no longer governed by what others think, but rather by what she knows to be true. This is a woman whose intuition is so well developed that she knows in her gut what to do, and part of her personal mission is to do things that are shaped by integrity, insight, and compassion. This woman can make things happen anywhere but, unlike the street-defined bitch, there is no selfishness, no harshness, no unkindness about her; she takes action and creates results that are in the highest and best interests of everyone involved, within the framework of wisdom and a love that goes beyond the human.

This may sound too good to be possible and, indeed, it is if we operate strictly from the limitations of personality and ego. But the Bitch has chosen to live from a deeper place; she has chosen, as a result of all she's learned, to be an expression of the Divine in everything she does. She has also learned, through the first half of life and all its experiences, to see both the big picture and the small pieces of any situation. Historically, women regarded as bitches were women who made things happen. They often did so in a fashion that caused pain and chaos, and their motivations were frequently self-serving. However, we can't ignore their ability to take action and create results. So, imagine the woman who is so personally powerful that things and people part before her like the Red Sea, and who is revered at the same time for being respectful, compassionate, and loving. Midlife is not intended to be an either/or event in which we must choose to be loved or to be effective. We get to be both, but it requires the willingness to remember who we really are, and to transform the negative beliefs and emotional barriers we've been carrying so we can live from the power that remains.

As mentioned earlier, the Bitch has learned to see situations in their Big Picture form, and then to break it down into manageable small pieces. This allows her to be both the visionary and the implementer. She can be consistently effective at both because she has come to trust her gut, and because she has learned to put emotion aside once she has determined what needs to be done. That doesn't mean she has no feelings as she uses her power. She has a great capacity to feel, but unchecked emotion can cloud her judgment; so once she is clear about the goal, her action is based on commitment. She doesn't waste time and energy wondering if she's made the right decision, if she's good enough to pull it off, or if someone else could do it better. She knows that second-guessing herself only dissipates her power and insight.

At fifty-eight, Dorothy felt confused, insignificant, and anxious. "I feel old and invisible. I don't know where I fit or who I'm supposed to be now. I guess it's part of getting older—I'm just not of much value any more. But why be alive if you have nothing to offer?" It was heartbreaking to hear her pain and to watch her struggle against tears that had probably built up over many years of neglect, loneliness, and fear. Her grown children, she went on to say, had always treated her like an afterthought, not unkind but also not aware of the depth possible in this woman they had learned to take for granted. At work, it was simply assumed that she would always be available to do whatever others didn't want to do, and her work went largely unnoticed. "It's okay," she assured me. "I don't need to be in the spotlight. I just wish I could feel like I matter somewhere."

But it wasn't okay, not really. Dorothy had a world of learning she could contribute, a number of opinions she only admitted to behind closed doors for fear they were the wrong ones, and several things she dreamed of doing but never had, having scared herself away from anything that wasn't familiar. "What if I'm too old, too stupid, too weak? What if there isn't enough money? What if I try something new and fail?" This had become her mantra and her prison.

Dorothy was an excellent example of a woman in need of Bitch energy. She had spent her life in the shadow of numerous other people, serving, nurturing, supporting—and becoming depleted in the process. In many respects, though she was nearing sixty, she was still unformed. Although she had opinions and dreams, she had never given herself permission to express, much less live, them. She had set herself up to feel insignificant through her willingness to fade into the background of life and stay there. All this could change, but only if she was willing to step out of the box her life had become and start to live out loud. As we worked together, she found options that allowed her to show up differently in her life, and learned to step into a state of calm from which she could access her own courage, power, and focus. She learned that she was much stronger than she had realized, and able to set a goal, recognize its meta-outcome, and take action. She developed an internal strategy for finding an unwavering focus, and for saying "no" when she needed to. As our work progressed, the timid, helpless, and uncertain woman who had initially contacted me began to be replaced by one who spoke with more authority, had more energy, and who felt at home in her own skin.

Dorothy called me three months after we had completed our work to report that she had told one of her kids not to interrupt her at a family gathering, and to treat her with respect from that time on. This had previously been unheard of, as it was her job to cook, serve, and clean up, not to be listened to. She had also spoken up at a church council meeting, calling for action on a serious matter and volunteering to head up a committee to remedy the situation. "They were shocked," she said. "I don't think I had ever spoken a word in those meetings, and here I was taking over and initiating change. I was nervous at first, but I knew it was the right thing to do and I didn't doubt that I could make it happen." Without raising her voice or behaving in an aggressive way contrary to her nature, this tiny, quiet, middle-aged woman had pointed out the path to resolution and rallied the group around her cause. There may have been those who resented her for requiring accountability and change, but this new Dorothy, this woman to contend with, was no longer shaped by their opinions.

The last time I heard from Dorothy, she had begun taking tango lessons and was planning a trip to Africa—simply because she'd always wanted to see it. In the past she had found the prospect overwhelming. Not any more.

Shawna learned as a child that a female's only power is sexual, and that the sole gauge of her value as a person was the amount of attention she got from men. This perspective made her a flirtatious little girl, and a dangerously seductive teenager. In her longing to feel valuable and cared for she used the only tool she thought she had, and for a while it seemed to work. At fifteen she was attracting men in their twenties. At seventeen she was pregnant, abandoned by both her family and the baby's father, and very alone. Realizing that a pregnant female is not considered sexy in the way she was used to, she quickly began resenting the child she was carrying, and ramped up her efforts to grab the attention she had begun to miss. The more evident her pregnancy became, the less seductive she appeared, and by the time she gave birth she was in a full-blown depression, which was made worse by alcohol. The only thing that had ever allowed her to feel powerful, her sexual demeanor, was no longer serving her, and she was left with no option but to feel worthless and insignificant. When she came to work with me, she was nearing fifty, ravaged by a lifetime of self-abuse, and bitter about an obvious lack of attention from men. Showing lots of cleavage, lots of leg, and wearing lots of makeup, she seemed to be hanging on desperately to the tools that had worked thirty years earlier. The difficulty now was that those tools were no longer getting her what she needed—the feeling of being wanted, important, and cared for. Shawna had moved into a time of life in which her inner power, if she knew how to use it, could create and attract everything she wanted, while the physical power she had once wielded had lost its edge.

Having never learned to explore herself as a multi-faceted individual, Shawna knew nothing of the deeper aspects of herself. In her sad and limited perception, all she had to offer was a nice body, a pretty face, and an impressive sex drive—and all those things had begun to change. The only gauge she had ever used to assess her value as a person had been the number of longing glances she got from men, and those glances had become rare. In order to make midlife a time of joy and possibility instead of depression and bitterness, she would have to be willing to find the aspects of herself that had been on hold. By continuing to think of herself as a twenty-year-old seductress, she drastically limited the opportunities available to her at this exceptional time of life. The behaviors that, at twenty, were considered sexy and cute are, at fifty, regarded as pathetic, inappropriate, and very sad. Shawna was faced with an uncomfortable choice—she could continue as she had been and find herself less respected and more alone, or she could choose to find the real woman who had been trapped inside her for so many years. She was being invited to explore unfamiliar territory, and she was scared.

Delores was a very different example of a woman who, at the midpoint of life, found herself at a crossroads, realizing that what used to get results was no longer working. Her high-powered career had begun immediately upon completing her MBA. At twenty-four, she was focused, regarded as an up-and-coming golden child, and already used to getting her own way. She had been courted by several large corporations, had essentially written her own ticket, and quickly began making things happen professionally. Over the years, as she moved through the ranks in a fast-paced corporate setting, Delores earned the title VP of International Operations—but behind her back she was known as the corporate Ball Buster. Her management style was reminiscent of various historical tyrants, only harsher. She routinely used intimidation to motivate employees, and was not opposed to hurling personal criticisms in order to leave people vulnerable and therefore easy to control. Men were a favorite target, and she was famous for exerting her considerable power, especially where they were concerned. She ran her personal life the same way she ran her business; she had few friends, and the ones she did have she managed to alienate early on in the relationship. Her dating experience was a kind of revolving door, with men coming and going quickly and breakups that were less than gracious.

Delores and I met when the president of her organization asked me to assess whether there was any hope of salvaging what had begun as a brilliant career, and devolved into a very sticky and unpleasant situation. "I don't want to lose her," he had said, "but she's become the person no one wants to be around. She's a strategic and technological genius, but I can't afford to lose any more people because she's so brutal. She's got thirty days to turn it all around, or I'll have to let her go." At that point Delores was fifty-three, alone, and living a life composed of nothing but work. Losing her job, the only thing by which she defined herself, would be devastating. And with her reputation for ruthlessness, it was unlikely that anyone else in her industry would take the risk of hiring her. Her dilemma was huge, and she didn't know it; her employer had asked me not to tell her about the thirty-day deadline. "She's very clever," he had said; "if she knows there's a deadline, she'll show you and me whatever we need to see in order to keep her job. If there's going to be a change, it has to be motivated by an authentic desire to operate differently, not by fear."

Before scheduling an initial session with Delores I needed more information. Was her current behavior different from the past, or just more of the same and worse? How long had her behaviors been this difficult? If she had always been this way, why had he waited so long to address the problem? How would he know that my work with Delores had been successful? His responses came quickly and readily. She had always been pushy and demanding, but "when she was younger and cuter, and an intriguing combination of beauty and balls" people had been more tolerant toward her. "She was young and eager, pretty, trying to make it up the ladder," he said shaking his head. "A lot of the men around here at that time saw her as a challenge; could they get next to her without losing their jobs? And if put to the test, could they be as tough as she was, could they get the job done like she did without stepping on important toes in the process? For the first few years it was exciting to try to keep up with her. Her tough energy, when she was young and sexy, was kind of charming. It isn't charming anymore." He went on to explain that over the years she had gotten harsher, more demanding, and several key people had threatened to leave the organization because she had become so difficult to deal with. "You'll have your hands full," he had warned, "but only for thirty days."

Our first meeting was unique and revealing. "What the hell am I here for?" she had bellowed at me as she entered my office, sat down, and put her feet up on my desk. She quickly backed down when I responded in a way that told her, respectfully, that she had met her match. With the jockeying for position out of the way, we got down to work. Early in our thirty-day time frame the situation became clear, and my heart went out to her. Delores had grown up with a powerful and successful father who routinely used fear to get what he wanted, and a weak and timid mother who was neglected, ridiculed, and occasionally used as a punching bag. When Delores left home for college, her mother had committed suicide. Growing up in such an environment, Delores learned that men were powerful and could make things happen, and women were weak and at the mercy of everything and everyone. If a woman aspired to power, she would have to behave like a man—only harder, louder, and with absolute inflexibility. Anything less would leave her vulnerable to the disrespect with which men regarded women. "I'll show the bastards" had become her personal and professional slogan, and her initial scramble up the corporate ladder had been done in a blaze of "screw you" glory.

But here she was, a middle-aged corporate executive with no friends, no meaningful relationships of any kind, and a bottomless pool of regret into which she dove periodically, swimming to save her life and hoping she could keep her head above the sorrow that threatened to drown her. I had seen this before: women who ignored their own natural instinct for connection and relationship in favor of the information and action form of power natural to men. Not that we have to choose one over the other; deeply and naturally powerful women gather information and take effective action because of and within the context of relationships they have formed and, ideally, continue to nurture. The opposite is true for men. In the course of gathering data and taking action, they can form connections and relationships. It's not an either/or proposition.

But with women like Delores, lines have blurred and things have become muddled. The conclusion they have drawn is that, in order to be a powerful and therefore emotionally indestructible individual, it must be necessary to live, work, and lead like a man. In order to pull this off, a woman has to intentionally ignore the urgings of her own nature (and hormones) to nurture and create connections. Because the information and action way of doing things feels less natural to a woman, as if a world of significant issues is being left out, women unaware of the power of their own essence often go overboard in their quest to live powerful lives.

In the case of Delores, she had found early in her career that she could put her natural inclination toward relationship on hold and instead focus on doing things the way she had learned from her father. Initially, this had generated impressive results, gotten her attention and a promotion, and people had found her interesting to banter with. What she hadn't realized was that, in large part, her steamroller style was tolerated because of the intriguing juxtaposition of her tougher-than-nails attitude and the obvious sexuality of an attractive, twenty-five-year-old woman. Over the course of her twenty-eight years with the company, that sexual attraction had begun to change. The men who had worked with her for many years had grown tired of her emasculating behaviors and learned to steer clear of her. The younger men feared and disliked her, and didn't find her sexually attractive; and the women avoided her as much as possible, unable to relate to her style, which they found to be cold and much more masculine than feminine. As she felt her external power slipping, Delores tightened her grip. Her "my way or the highway" style had worked in the past, and she was determined to make sure it continued to work. To that end, she became more of everything she had already been—more demanding, more intimidating, more critical, more threatening. The harder she pushed, the more her power failed her. Since she was no longer the intriguing, sexy twenty-five-year-old, people related to her solely on the basis of her behaviors, which had become intolerable. Without her sexuality and the beauty of youth to cushion the blow, her colleagues saw her as she really was—insecure, mean-spirited, and bitter. The time had come for a major decision: She could continue down this path and quickly find herself unemployed and even more alone, or she could learn to recognize and implement the true power she carried as a woman. This would require a huge shift in perspective and behavior, and I wasn't sure she was up to it.

Both Shawna and Delores had lived the first half of their lives with a distorted understanding of a woman's power and how it can best be used. This distortion had resulted in lives filled with loneliness, confusion, and disappointment. Had these two lovely women chosen to explore and value the nature of their true power, the first part of life could have been much more rewarding. That inherent power is the true expression of the Bitch.

At midlife, the Bitch has come to recognize, take possession of, and revel in the remarkable power women carry. She has also committed herself to using her power to create results that serve the highest and best for everyone involved. This awareness and commitment indicate a very different inner state than that of the women who, historically, have either recognized their power and abused it, or who were unaware of the power they carried, and therefore lived in the shadow of others, often feeling hopeless and resentful. The power manifested by the Bitch is not based on external factors—title, money, authority, appearance—but rather on who she has come to be as, through the rigors of the first half of life, she has grown into her own soul. The Bitch lives the integration of personal power and compassion, and the balance between the two is unwavering.

Delores is a stunning example of the transformation that can take place when a woman chooses to become the Bitch. Within our thirty-day timeframe she learned to forgive herself, her father, and her mother, and to experience what life is like for her employees. She came to understand, for the first time, the damage she had done by attacking others, and the degree to which fear was a dubious motivator. And most importantly, she began to see herself from an elevated perspective and to grasp the fact that sorrow and loneliness had formed her behavior. "Is it time to change all this?" I asked as we moved toward our thirty-day deadline. "Yes," she said quietly but firmly. "I want to change. Please help me." My final meeting with Delores happened at her office. She had asked me to be there when she called in everyone in her department and, in front of the entire group, asked their forgiveness. "I've been an unkind and intolerant manager," she said, fighting tears. "I want to be a different kind of person and boss. Please help me as I change." I'm sure there were no dry eyes in the room as people spoke up, offering support. One month later, the gentleman who had initially asked me to work with her called me. "I don't know what the two of you did during those thirty days," he said in a tone verging on disbelief, "but whatever it is, it worked. We don't ever want to lose Delores. She's like a completely different person. People are asking to be moved *into* her department instead of out." What happened during those remarkable thirty days was the transformation from scared, lonely, and insecure woman to true Bitch. This was a shift that changed everything.

Shawna is still exploring the aspects of herself that had never before been expressed. She's taking classes in things she once would have found dull, has begun working with an image consultant to help her dress more appropriately, and is working hard at providing herself the attention, love, and respect she thought could only come from men. She called me recently to tell me about a paper she had written for a class, which the professor asked to read to the entire group. She was excited, and I was momentarily concerned that her excitement came from the attention this brought her. "No," she said, "I just felt so surprised that something I did, thoughts I had, were important enough to be noticed. It wasn't the attention I liked, it was realizing that I have something to offer I hadn't been aware of." This was a big step toward trusting and honoring herself. Shawna is well on her way toward the wonderful world of the Bitch.

The Bitch's power to make things happen in a way that does no harm has a five-pronged foundation:

1. An authentic desire to be of service

2. A profound longing to live as an expression of the Divine

3. A deep self-awareness and respect; the ability to always know and honor what is true for her

4. A way of showing up in the world that reflects values and convictions to which she is unshakably committed

5. A spiritual clarity that allows her to see beyond the surface to the deeper aspects of any situation

An exceptional example is the grandmother of a friend of mine. When I met her, she was in her mid-seventies and had only been in the United States a few years. Her earlier life in her own country had been rigorous and demanding: She had married at sixteen, had her first child at seventeen, and over the next ten years had borne six more babies, two of whom had died in infancy. There had been little money, but a tremendous amount of love and joy amid lots of hardship. Her intense faith was a mix of Catholicism, shamanism, and a touch of folklore, and it had shaped her response to all her experiences and made her a fierce and loving woman. She found great delight in being of service to others, and she saw God in everything and everyone. No one in her presence ever felt inadequate or unimportant, and she could draw out the most introverted individual and leave him feeling listened to, understood, and cared for. But as kind and loving as she was, she was not to be messed with—no one ever crossed this five-foot-tall, 100-pound, wrinkled old woman. She did not tolerate unkindness or deception, would not allow anyone to speak disparagingly of him or herself, and immediately shut down any attempts at gossip. Her behavior sprang from an unwavering sense of what was right and true. With very little formal education, no knowledge of business or finance, no impressive title, and absolutely no pretense about her, this tiny old woman commanded awe and respect everywhere she went. It was her very essence, her presence that allowed her to make things happen. I never heard her raise her voice, never saw her judging others or playing on people's fears to get what she wanted. And yet, wherever she went, her power was palpable. I doubt that she ever thought of herself as a powerful woman; she was simply very present in every authentic moment of her life.

All five essential elements of the power of the Bitch have their beginning in the power of relationship—to one's spiritual Source, to one's true Self, and to other living beings as spiritual kin. With those relationships in place, the elements of true power become a way of being.

The desire to be of service is a gift when it comes from a clean intention. The difficulty is that such a desire can and often does have an agenda that is anything but altruistic. The intention behind the desire governs the choices made and the actions taken, and can result in outcomes that are as suspect as the intention itself.

Cheryl prided herself on her metaphysical approach to life and the ways in which she was of service to the community. She had left a lucrative corporate position to open a healing center, and provided books, tapes, and other spiritually focused tools for those who were seeking a sacred path. She brought in speakers who could illuminate spiritual concepts, and held frequent workshops for individuals interested in exploring various metaphysical activities. Her center was popular, her events well attended, and she became the Grande Dame of the local metaphysical community.

After several years of financial success and high visibility, things began to spiral downward in a most revealing way. A shaky economy had negatively affected sales, and several long-term customers had begun spending time at a new center where products and services were less expensive. Rumor had it that the employees at Cheryl's center were planning to leave and open a center of their own. "How could they do this to me after everything I've done for them?" she asked in a snarling sort of whine. "Whatever happened to loyalty? Not only my employees, but my customers, too—nobody has appreciated me or all my effort the way they should have. They should be grateful for everything I've done for them. Instead, this is the thanks I get. They can go to hell for all I care."

As I listened, I remembered something the Buddha said, that expectation is the mother of disappointment. Cheryl had entered into her business venture and the relationships it involved with the expectation that her efforts would be met with appreciation and gratitude, and that both would come in the form that would be most meaningful to her. Her desire to be of service was in place only as long as those she served responded in a particular way. When what she had expected was not forthcoming, her true motivation had shown itself.

"Is that why you opened your center, to get appreciation and recognition from people who use your products and services?" I asked. "Well," she stammered, "of course not. I opened the business in order to help the community. I wanted to serve others."

"Cheryl," I responded, aware of how hurt her feelings had been, "if your intention was to be of service, you can find great peace in the knowledge that you have, indeed, done that. We both know of many people who found solace and even direction at your facility. You have even been of service to your employees by teaching them so well that they can open their own business. You have met the goal of being of service in those ways, and you can afford to move on to the next form of service. If, however, your intention was to receive recognition and to be appreciated, then you have put your sense of your own value in the hands of others, and you leave yourself no option but to be disappointed in the people who haven't met your expectation. It may be time to get very clear about the true nature of your intention, so you can take direct action to get what you really want. You see," I continued, "as long as you have to depend on external sources to give you what you need, you are not in control of your own life. Someone else is running your show while you wait for whatever they happen to offer. This is a passive and powerless approach to life, and you deserve to make your life happen rather than waiting for it to happen to you."

For Cheryl, her stated intention (to be of service) and the way she went about it (opening a healing center) masked a deeper need. She had hoped that her center, as important as it had been in the community, would get her what she hadn't been able to give herself—love, respect, and a feeling of importance.

As long as we live in human bodies and on a very human planet, we can't entirely escape the needs of the ego. To varying degrees, people need to feel cared for, valued, and significant, and most of us spend a lot of time and energy seeking those responses from others. There is nothing shameful or selfish about wanting this; however, the Bitch has learned that the way it's gone about will determine the extent to which she can find satisfaction. She has learned to live with a constant internal source of love, respect, and value, and to look for whatever she needs from sources outside herself in ways that are honest, open, and straightforward. And she does this without hurting anyone. That may sound like a tall assignment, and it merits an examination of her strategy and technique.

Most of us (including those who step into Bitch mode at midlife) learn as children that it's very important to please others in order to be included and accepted in our families, our peer groups, and our communities. Frequently, and often beginning in childhood, there is an almost irrational fear of being alone or excluded. This anxiety commonly leads potentially extraordinary people to camouflage their own natures in favor of behaviors and philosophies that will make them more acceptable to those who make the social rules of a particular group. This probably has to do, at least in part, with the fact that human beings are social creatures and can thrive on the companionship of others; however, this powerful and sometimes desperate need to belong and to be accepted may also be an unconscious throwback to ancient times, when being rejected or excluded from the tribe often meant certain death.

There are numerous allusions in both history and myth to ancient cultures rejecting and exiling individuals who had violated the laws of the group. Members of the tribe or clan turned their backs on the violator, leaving him to fend for himself without the resources or the protection of the group. This was an early—and much more dangerous—form of the shunning used today by some religious and even social groups to punish those who don't conform or fit in. Whereas contemporary shunning is a psychological and emotional form of discipline, being put outside the camp in ancient times often also meant no access to food, water, or protection from the elements or predators. Along with the emotional pain of rejection by one's community came the virtual guarantee of a terrifying and painful death. In light of this, it was considered essential to live by the rules and to be found pleasing by those who were in positions of power. It was a matter of personal safety.

This is significant because, although today rejection by others rarely results in death, the fear of being rejected or excluded remains. Although this may have to do with the emotional need for connection held by most people, there is a difference between wanting genuine relationship and wanting to avoid rejection. So, why does this drive to be accepted by others remain, even though we no longer have to fear the terror and death exclusion used to bring? And why is this anxiety not an issue for the Bitch?

The feeling of connection—to another person or to a group— brings with it a sense of safety. There is somewhere to turn, someone who will help, and somewhere we are wanted or at least tolerated. We have not been left alone to face the sometimes-hard edges of life. Most of us learned as children about fitting in and doing whatever it took to be included. But for many, the process of creating relationships with others took priority over the much more fundamental process of creating relationship with ourselves. We formed our sense of who we are, what we deserve, and what's possible from the opinions and impressions of others instead of through an ongoing journey into our own depth of excellence. This leaves us vulnerable, on an emotional roller coaster. When the people around us treat us well, we feel good about ourselves; when they treat us badly or are indifferent to us, we may crash emotionally and often increase our efforts to find an indication, from sources outside ourselves, that we are safe and okay.

Being at the mercy of those whose approval we seek is a product of having neglected to form the more reliable bonds between ourselves and both Spirit and our deeper Self. Clearly, people need to feel loved, respected, cared for. If I don't yet know how to be a source of those things for myself, I have to go somewhere outside myself to find them. The quickest way is to become what others want me to be in order to be accepted as one of them. There are three very high prices to pay for this: I don't get to explore my own remarkable nature, I constantly give myself the message that who I really am isn't adequate, and I have to be vigilant to avoid blowing my cover and revealing that I may be someone different than they think I am. This is an exhausting, disrespectful, and deceptive way to live.

The Bitch has moved beyond this quandary, having spent time there, having found it to be a place of emotional and spiritual quicksand, and having learned that the harder she struggled for approval from others, the less authentic she became. The less authentic she became, the less trustworthy her intentions were. When everything she did had at its foundation the need for approval and recognition from others, stated intentions like "being of service" were immediately suspect. Did she really want to be of service, or was being of service just another way to get approval? After spending a huge amount of time and energy in an exhausting scramble to be good enough, and having reached a point at which she said "enough," Cheryl found a better way. By becoming her own ongoing source of the love, respect, and approval, and by choosing to see herself as valuable, worthwhile, and deserving of love and joy, she launched a new way of showing up in the world.

This shift that placed her firmly in the realm of the Bitch took some work. After having spent most of her time and energy focused on the opinions and judgments of others, it was time to get acquainted with her own. For the first half of her life, Cheryl had been so concerned with the impressions of others that she neglected to form any for herself. She may have lived a chameleon-like existence, changing the shape of her feelings, thoughts, attitudes, and behaviors to fit each situation she found herself in, and never taking her own unique shape. At midlife, however, the angst and emptiness that came with not knowing who she really was became too great a burden, and she began to explore the things that were true for her. In the process, she was able to discern the fundamental or meta-outcomes underlying her intentions, and to face the aspects of her life in which she needed to be more real with love and diligence.

This isn't always a comfortable process. It takes courage to look honestly at yourself, accept what you find, and take action to shore up the places where you want to be stronger. Many people avoid this process, afraid of what they'll find in honestly exploring their true nature; but, in reality, the gift offered in this process is the discovery of the exceptional person living within. Developing a deep and intimate relationship with yourself opens the door to a whole parade of extraordinary and unexpected experiences, and brings with it a new awareness of your kinship to the Divine.

A woman becomes the Bitch when she recognizes the Divine within herself: the place at her core, in her essence, where there is great peace; a place with no mind chatter, no fear, and profound clarity; a place from which she can take action that aligns with everything sacred and honorable. When operating from that place, her intentions become clean and clear, she is grounded and centered, her power is unmistakable, and everything is possible.

Cheryl's need for validation was great, and it took a while before she could even think in terms of giving herself recognition and appreciation. "What if you had value simply because you exist?" I asked. "What if you could see and feel that value and cherish yourself whether anyone else did or not? How would life be then?"

"It would be wonderful," she responded. "But it doesn't make any sense. How can I have value if I haven't done anything significant? I have to earn it; I know I matter when I see that other people find me important. Otherwise I'm nobody."

Cheryl's entire frame of reference was external, and as a result she had lived her whole life in reactive mode, hostage to the attitudes of others. Now, in her late forties, with a failing business, no meaningful relationships to speak of, and the prospect of having to start over looming large, it had become clear that if she remained dependent on others for a sense of well-being, the disappointment, bitterness, and lack of self-respect would erode any possibility of happiness. Without a stronger sense of self, she had no way to form authentic intentions or take honest action; everything she did was motivated by her need for the approval of others in order to feel better about herself.

Cheryl's inability to provide for herself emotionally is not unusual. Many people live with the opinions of others as their only gauge of self-worth. Like so many others, Cheryl had never created a loving and nurturing relationship within, so in a very real sense she was a stranger to herself. Before she could live an authentic life and create intentions without hidden agendas, she would have to fall in love with herself. Loving herself would bring numerous elements to her everyday experience. Self-respect, integrity, passion, and the moment-to-moment opportunity to feel loved, valuable, and worthy would combine to form a new way of being for her, should she choose to begin the sacred, sometimes scary, journey to the Self.

Talk is cheap when it comes to self-love, especially in times when terms like "new age" and "spiritual" are casual parts of everyone's vocabulary. It's often much easier to talk about loving oneself and nurturing one's own soul than it is to actually do it. And, unless we've had good role models, the whole idea of clean intentions beginning with self-love may be confusing and a bit mysterious. So, let's define our terms. On one hand, it's very simple. Think of someone you love deeply (not out of neediness or co-dependence, or any other unhealthy connection), and the way you care for, protect, nurture, support, and show compassion to that individual. How does it compare to the way you treat yourself? For most of us, the comparison is painfully revealing because, on the other hand, we tend to see ourselves through a lens made up of all the things we have come to believe make us unworthy. Mistakes we've made, relationships we handled poorly, lies, betrayals, perceived failures, deceptions in which we played a part, all of these contribute to our concept of who we are and what we deserve. The way we see ourselves determines the degree to which we are able to develop self-respect, self-love, and a sense of ourselves as valuable beings.

Under all the new age glitz, and her presentation of herself as a community benefactor, Cheryl saw herself as fundamentally unworthy of love and respect. She was unable to live from a clean intention to be of service because she was certain that someone as unworthy as herself was not powerful or important enough to truly be of service. Her painful lack of self-love and respect left her no option but to search constantly for signs that others found her adequate.

For the Bitch, however, loving herself and being real is a given. She can't be a true Bitch without it. It begins with the understanding that who she is right now is okay, flaws and all. She doesn't have to reach perfection (or prove her sincerity by sweating blood in the process) in order to deserve joy. And once she has seen herself in the bright and revealing light of love, she immediately becomes responsible for cleaning up her messes and getting on track without the debilitating effects of guilt or shame. Avoiding that cleanup process is no longer an option, now that she has taken stock and begun to realize who she really is. From that point on, the Bitch lives a life based on her knowledge of herself as a creature sprung from the Divine, already carrying everything she needs to be extraordinary. "I am a woman of depth, integrity, honesty, and compassion, and I choose to express all that in every situation" becomes her mantra, and her true and sacred nature, from that point forward, is obvious to all.

There are many benefits that come with learning to like, love, and nurture yourself. The grandest and most far-reaching is that it loosens the emotional tangles that occur when our state of mind hinges on what other people think. When I am no longer entangled with others in a powerless way, I am able to see the bigger picture of all the aspects of my life. And besides all that, when I like who I am, life feels much better.

No longer willing to feel resentful and lonely, Cheryl decided to wade into herself and test the waters. Nervous but determined, she began the process of forming an intimate relationship with her real self, and life as she had always known it started to change. We launched the shift very simply, with an ongoing exercise in gratitude (the most powerful state available to humans), followed by several sessions during which she practiced seeing herself from different perspectives, seeing experiences she regretted from a place of forgiveness, stepping into wisdom and integrity, and forming her take on the future from that inner state. Over the course of several weeks, our work together moved more and more deeply into Cheryl's heart and soul, and I marveled at how, with each piece of work we did, she seemed more grounded, more at home within her own spirit. She was shedding her old persona, and someone remarkable was beginning to emerge.

It's been several months since we completed our work. I ran into Cheryl on the street recently, and learned that she's taken a job that has her much less in the forefront of things than before, and much more serene. "I enjoy what I'm doing," she said; "I know I'm helping people in a quiet way, and I'm at peace with it. It no longer seems important for other people to think so highly of me. I think I've learned to like who I am." Her intention to be of service is now sincere and has become a way of life, not a means to an end. The transformation was lovely.

The profound longing to live as an expression of the Divine springs directly from the power of relationship. Until we have come to know the sacred realm and to explore our connection to the Source, "spiritual" remains only a concept, and everything we have to offer is limited by our very human nature. When, in any situation, I present only my own personal love, there is a limited amount of it to go around. In the face of various circumstances (betrayal, deception, hurt feelings, insensitivity, even boredom), I may find that the love I felt has changed to anger, resentment, fear, or indifference. This transmutation shifts the nature of the relationship, and what was once a source of joy and passion becomes a burden. There are four kinds of love, referred to in several sacred texts and by numerous spiritual writers and teachers. The writer C.S. Lewis presents them succinctly in his book *The Four Loves*:

1. Eros, romantic love

2. Philia (or filia), the bond of friendship

3. Storgeo, the love of family

4. Agape, the unconditional love of God

The element shared among the first three is that of self-interest. Eros love drives us to "have" another person in order to feel something we aren't feeling otherwise. Philia love is based on the sharing of things in common: I love you and want you as a friend because you are like me and, around you, I don't feel so alone in the world. Storgeo love is a bond based on love of one's own genetic material: I love you because you and I share the same basic genetic makeup and I recognize a bit of myself in you. This is not cold, just human. We have a strong, even primitive drive to survive both physically and emotionally, and each of these types of love has that drive at its foundation.

Because they are so strong, eros, philia, and storgeo can feel unconditional and eternal in the throes of a powerful romantic encounter, a close and meaningful experience with a friend, or a family situation in which everyone works together toward a common goal. But in truth, the only love that has no end is agape, the love of the Divine. Consider the former romantic partner who at the time seemed to give meaning to life, but whose name you now struggle to remember; or the friend you haven't spoken to for months or years because of a falling out; or the family member whose attitudes and behaviors have eroded any interest you may have had in spending time together. No matter how vigorous our human love may seem at the time, it can come to an end. The love of Spirit or God does not depend on our behavior, our attitude, or our following somebody's rules. Because the Divine is constant in Its very nature, Its love is constant and unconditional.

Agape love is not a mushy or self-interested; it's not a defensive or vindictive love, but instead a rigorous love that requires the best of each of us and loves everything that falls short as well. There are no messy entanglements that result from expressing and receiving Divine love—no regret, no hurt feelings, no neediness. Becoming a conduit for the love of the Divine allows the Bitch to carry with her into all situations a love that heals and transforms.

Several years ago I traveled to an area of extreme poverty in Asia, and came away devastated by what I had seen. The starvation, the frequent deaths of babies, homeless people, and animals—all this had wrenched my heart, leaving me with the need to do something to help and the knowledge that I couldn't fix the situation. I felt such concern for all the life forms there that were suffering, and my emotional energy was drained by the haunting images I couldn't seem to shake. At lunch one day I mentioned this to a very wise friend who said "You are sending your own love to this place; that will exhaust and deplete you and won't do them any good. Always send the love of God, not your human love, when a situation demands transformation." I was both shaken and relieved by what she said, and the wisdom of her words has stayed with me all these years. I was shaken because her statement forced me to look at my own capacity for love. My human love has limitations and flaws, and is a self-interested love. I love because it feels good to do so (or bad, but in a self-interested way), because connecting with someone can be rewarding to me, because my link to someone has a genetic component and so I recognize something of myself in that person. When it no longer feels good (or rewardingly bad) or is convenient to love, I will most likely stop loving. I was relieved by my friend's insight because it helped to lift the burden of having to love everything and everyone in a way I, on my own, am not capable of. When I allow the love of the Divine to move through me toward others, I am offering them something eternal and unwavering, something I cannot offer on my own.

The only way we can live as expressions of the Divine is to become acquainted with that Source. We can't express what we aren't familiar with. Once the Bitch has begun to recognize the presence, power, and love of Source, which is grander than herself, she can no longer seek the recognition of others as she once did; human applause pales in comparison to alignment with the Divine. The process of making the acquaintance of the Sacred often starts small: noticing the small and quiet indications of something too beautiful to have sprung solely from human hands; the occasional "peak experiences," a term coined by Abraham Maslow to describe times, often only for a moment, when everything feels perfectly congruent and aligned; and certainly the awareness of something pure and hopeful in one's own heart. As the Bitch experiences the power and love of the Sacred, she discovers a deep desire to carry that power and love into everything. It is so clean and so constant that it is a joy to convey.

Just as is the case where love is concerned, our personal capacity for compassion, forgiveness, wisdom, and power is greatly limited by the size and shape of our human nature. As with love, our own ability to be compassionate, forgiving, wise, and powerful is tainted and restricted by the ego needs to which we are all subject while having this human experience. Like love, compassion, forgiveness, wisdom, and power all have that same self-serving element, and are all liable to come to an end—sometimes quickly, sometimes over long and drawn out periods—when they no longer serve us. The Bitch cannot afford to operate from that place of limitation; she can only function with true power when that power springs from a vaster place.

Because she has come to realize that the source of her power lies far beyond herself, the Bitch no longer tries to fool herself and others into believing that her extraordinary nature is of her own making. Having long since given up both arrogance and self-deprecating behavior, the Bitch operates from the unparalleled humility and joy that come with knowing that she is being used for a profound purpose. The more space she clears within, the more space the Divine has to flow into and through, healing, transforming, and empowering both the Bitch as conduit and those around her in the process.

The Bitch lives a grounded, balanced, and practical life; she must do so, or she's in danger of becoming what my mother has referred to as so heavenly minded she's no earthly good. There is nothing noble about saying all the right things while living in a way that negates all those righteous and honorable words. I once heard a spiritual teacher say to someone "Don't tell me what you believe and what's important to you. For one day, let me watch how you live, where you put your time and energy, how you speak to and treat others and yourself, and then I will tell you what you believe and what you value." Talk is cheap when it comes to power and spirituality, and anyone can learn the lingo. The real test is in how well one's spirituality is demonstrated in the day-to-day, mundane life. The true Bitch applies the spark of the Divine, carried in her soul, to her daily life and finds that, when touched by that sacred power, everything changes. This is what makes her the Bitch—she lives both the power and the love simultaneously.

The deep longing to live as an expression of the Divine is generated when she begins to recognize the enormity of what it means to carry the Divine nature within. As she experiences the unchanging love of Spirit, as she more frequently notices myriad indications of the presence of something holy in her daily routine, as she reflects on compassion that knows no bounds, the desire to be a transmitter of these things and the healing they bring becomes her driving force. In the process of expressing the nature of the Divine, the Bitch takes action in all areas of her life, which results in significant outcomes without doing harm.

The Bitch is a woman whose perspective has grown from small and self-serving to vast and unencumbered. Unlike the garden-variety bitch, whose goals and actions originate in a kind of tunnel vision that prevents her from seeing anything beyond what she wants, the divine Bitch has developed an immense field of vision, and chooses her actions, words, and projects with the highest good as her primary criterion. While careening through that sometimes treacherous first half of life, she has learned to look at life from that slightly elevated plane that makes it possible to perceive and understand things that are elusive when she is in the midst of circumstances. It is from that higher viewpoint that she can see the complex fabric of a situation, and how all its parts fit together to form the whole. Because she feels deeply for the small pieces as well as the whole, she can choose action that benefits all.

The Bitch is all about action, making life happen in a way that honors everyone because it honors and expresses the Divine. A client of mine was a great example of this. Roberta came to work with me because of an overwhelming challenge at work. Her company had merged with one of their biggest competitors, and the tension between the two sets of employees was palpable. Employees of Roberta's company were angry because they were being asked to welcome people they regarded as threats, and employees from the other organization were upset at being required to move to a location that was someone else's territory, and being forced into positions that were, in several cases, not at all what they had been hired to do. There was a clear "us versus them" feel to the place, and productivity had fallen dramatically. Passive-aggressive behavior had affected the quality of work, and as a result customers were beginning to leave.

As VP of the company, Roberta was being tasked with handling this chaos—and the president of the firm had told her that it would be fine with him if she just got rid of everybody involved in the turf war and started over with new people. She wasn't willing to scrap the training that had been provided to those employees, nor was she willing to let go of any of the new people she hadn't yet gotten to know. But she also knew that things couldn't continue as they were. They would eventually lose not only good customers, but also good employees.

"I don't know what to do," she told me. "I know I have to take action, but whatever I do it will piss somebody off. I feel paralyzed." Her frustration was evident, and I knew that if she considered her situation from only one perspective, someone was bound to lose when she finally took action.

The Bitch knows how to explore a variety of perspectives, including one from a higher plane, in order to find a solution that fits cleanly, so I knew that Roberta had to do the same. I asked her first to set in her own heart the intention to honor everyone in the situation. This alone lightened the burden she had been carrying, allowing her to be equally concerned about every person she was dealing with.

Next, I showed Roberta how to step into the experience of each group of people who would be affected by the action she took. As she temporarily took on the feelings and viewpoint of the employees who had been with her company for some time and who were threatened by the new people, she had a whole new appreciation for what the situation was doing to them. Shaking off that position, she moved into the experience of the new people, who were on new turf where everything they had accomplished elsewhere was of little import. I could see on her face the impact this had on her. The process I asked her to move through had opened her eyes and given her an emotional understanding of their circumstance, instead of leaving her with a solely intellectual grasp. She then shook off that experience and became, for a moment, the people in management in both companies, adding yet another dimension to the equation. I then asked her to look at the state of affairs from an elevated place, like a neutral observer watching from a point above the situation. This allowed her to see everything and everyone at the same time, and to notice how it could all fit together. Finally, I asked her to return to her own viewpoint, bringing with her all the information she had gained from each of the positions she had taken. The process had expanded her view of the complex situation in which she and her company found themselves, and from this new place she found that several ideas presented themselves immediately. Because she had explored the positions of every group affected, she could easily evaluate each option to ensure that it would work, at least on some level, for everyone. Understanding, at a gut level, how each faction was feeling opened the door to creative possibilities that hadn't been available to her when her perspective was one-sided and intellectual.

Her solution was both inspired and resourceful. She met with each group, shared with them her intention to respect everyone in the action she took, and proceeded to brainstorm with them about the needs they had and their ideas for making the transition as smooth and as comfortable as possible. She was delighted to find that in each group there were individuals with great ideas that hadn't occurred to her, and that she could add to her list of choices. Once she had compiled lists from each of the groups, she formed teams made up of people from both sides and gave them the assignment to come up with at least three workable options from those lists for creating a new organization that effectively used the skills, experience, and past accomplishments of the employees from both companies. The teams were asked to do at least some of their work together offsite, over lunch or perhaps at breakfast on the weekend, in order to begin to know each other as human beings instead of just interlopers or threats. They met each other's families, heard each other's stories, and began to see the things they had in common. All the while, they were operating as teams with a common goal: to find a way to make an unwelcome merger benefit not only the new entity and its management, but its employees as well. Within only a couple of weeks the atmosphere in the place had begun to change, and ninety days later an option was selected and quickly implemented. By the time all this had happened, things at the company had started to feel almost seamless, as if the two groups had always been a team.

The action Roberta had taken, from initial intention through implementation of the selected option, had resulted in the desired outcome without disrespecting or rolling over anyone, not even the lowest-paid employee. Productivity increased dramatically, morale improved, and the bottom line was enhanced quickly. And most importantly to Roberta, the employees liked being there. This is the Bitch at her best, making things work and creating results that matter without doing damage in the process.

All other elements that form the foundation for the Bitch's power-without-harm emanate from these first two. It is in looking at her human nature through the eyes of the Divine that she has developed a deep self-awareness, self-respect, and the ability to honor what's true for her everywhere she goes. The Bitch has neither the time nor the inclination to judge herself or others; there are far too many other, much more useful things to spend her energy on. Instead, she observes, responds with a rigorous kind of compassion, takes action when appropriate, and moves on. Her mission, living as an expression of the Divine, is always at the center of her awareness and is the motivation behind the way she lives. Her way of showing up in the world reflects the values and convictions to which she is unshakably committed, and these values and convictions, born of her intimate connection to her spiritual Source, are what determine the actions she takes. This is more than the "what would Jesus do?" fad of several years ago when, by asking themselves that question, individuals felt they could quickly find actions and responses most acceptable to God. There is nothing wrong with the question, except that it assumes that the deepest and most spiritually whole and pure responses can be found through the limited capacity of the human mind. We can't think our way to alignment with Spirit; we must *become* that alignment. Because while in the midst of our human experience we cannot entirely escape the needs of the ego, when we *think* about the right action to take, we can be sure that our decision will be tainted by our humanness. This means that we'll be tripping over our own hidden agendas no matter how pure we think our motives are. The Bitch has learned, while still in the body, to open herself to the power of the Divine in order to take actions that spring from that pure Source. This is the Bitch as a channel for the Sacred.

The final of the five elements of her power is the spiritual clarity that allows her to see beyond the surface to the deeper aspects of any situation. This is crucial to the Bitch, as without it she is destined to respond routinely to the surface behaviors of others rather than to the deeper underlying motivations behind those behaviors. This results in responding from a place of superficial understanding and insecurity.

A colleague of mine has told me often about her mentor, who is a remarkable woman. "She never just lashes out when people are rude or unkind," she marvels. "She doesn't tolerate disrespectful behavior, but before responding she looks for the possible deeper reasons for a person's actions. That lets her feel concern for the other person rather than anger or defensiveness, and her reactions are much kinder and more effective even when she has to confront the behavior." I remember one story in particular, which took place when my friend's mentor was Christmas shopping in a large mall. There was only one cashier and a long line of customers, and the employee was overtly brusque and impatient with each customer whose turn it was to pay for purchases.

Customers were responding with their own defensiveness, which seemed only to make things worse. As she stood in line observing the other woman's unprofessional behavior, my colleague's mentor asked herself what might be motivating such harshness. As she examined the kinds of things that could be the basis for such actions, she could only feel compassion for the woman at the register. When it was her turn she found herself subjected to the angst of the cashier and said, "I think you must be going through some difficult things right now to be so unkind to people. I hope that, whatever the unhappy situations are that you're in, you'll be able to find the best possible solution without having to hurt other people in the process. If I can help you move through this challenging time, please let me know." With that, she handed the woman her card and prepared to take her purchases and leave. At that moment the cashier reached out, took her hand, and began to cry. "My husband died two weeks ago, and I don't know how to go on. Christmas was always such a wonderful time for us, and without him everything feels empty and dark. I'm sorry I was rude to you. I'm just so lonely." It was a huge lesson for everyone in line who heard and observed what went on. Her personal despair explained her behavior, but did not excuse it. Her actions were unacceptable, but what she needed most immediately was compassion, not defensiveness from others. The ability and willingness of my friend's mentor to look beyond the surface to the deeper reason allowed her to offer that compassion while gently pointing out to the woman that the way she had chosen to express her unhappiness was inappropriate. The mentor's skill at intuiting a deeper need, her respectful response to rude behavior, and the unexpected offer of help combined to open the heart of this newly-widowed woman so she could begin to heal. This is the Bitch in action—responding to the root of any situation rather than its surface manifestation.

There are two additional, important points to make about the Bitch. This is a woman with an edge to her—not a defensive or vengeful edge, but an edge all the same. She is not moved to the kind of anger that festers and then erupts inappropriately, because she is clear about what needs to be done and is the first one to take action. Resentment and gossip are not part of her world, where everything is focused on highest and best action. However, this is not a woman to cross. While the Bitch often has an inherent sweetness to her, springing from her appreciation of life and her awareness of the presence of the Divine, hers is not a powerless or docile sweetness; she knows when it's time, from her larger-than-life spirit, to holler "*enough*," and bring unacceptable and unjust activities to a swift end. This has nothing to do with physical stature, legal authority, or the possession of small weapons. This has everything to do with the fact that the Bitch can bore through all the less-than-honest nonsense in any circumstance right to the heart of things, and from a deeper realm requires that life be honored. She is a fierce woman, not savage or uncivilized, but unwavering in her commitment to the Sacred in all its manifestations. She can take righteous offense at anything that denies the divine nature of every living thing. And if that happens, her response will be quick and definitive.

The other important aspect of this extraordinary woman is that she is able to be the Bitch because her focus has changed. During the first part of her life, most of her attention and energy was likely spent on forging relationships and forming people's impressions of who she was and what she was capable of. She scrutinized much, if not most, of her behavior ahead of time to ensure that it would be acceptable to those she valued. This may often have meant that things she wanted to do or say were left undone or unsaid because of the possible negative response from others. For this reason, whole aspects of herself may not have been given expression when she was younger, resulting in much of the angst she probably felt as she stumbled reluctantly toward midlife.

But now things have changed. Somehow, as we begin wrapping up the earlier period of our lives, most of us find ourselves no longer so concerned about the popular opinion. I'm not entirely certain how this happens, but there seem to be several things that influence us in that direction. Some of us, having been around a while, have noticed that the viewpoints and preferences that are popular and widely held at any given moment tend to be fickle and fleeting. My fashion sense may be considered very cool today, and totally uncool next month. The same is true of everything in my experience. My political views may be in favor now, and not so much later. My parenting skills may seem pretty good, until somebody writes a book that says I'm ruining my child. Trying hard to be in favor with most people all of the time involves a lot of ups and downs and frequent and sudden changes that all make for a very bumpy ride. Perhaps at midlife we have just gotten tired of the emotional motion sickness that comes with having to bounce all over the map in an attempt to keep up.

Another, somewhat sadder possibility is that many of us may no longer expect to be accepted, approved of, or considered valuable. If this is the case, those feeling this way may reason, "What do I care what others think about what I do? They don't think I matter anyway, so what do I have to lose?" This is an "it can't get any worse" approach that tends to form when a woman feels there is simply nothing left to lose by doing what she wants to do. It takes a long time to reach that point, and every moment spent moving sluggishly toward that depth of despair is a moment that can't be recaptured.

The third possible explanation for why women at midlife are often no longer caught up in the murky waters of public opinion is that, through everything that makes the first half of life what it is, they may have learned to trust themselves. Every time they took action that worked or that taught them something, every time they did something that made a difference, every time they chose the high road instead of something less honorable, their trust in themselves has been strengthened. Recognizing that those younger and less experienced are still being formed, and don't have all the answers, women at midlife (and beyond) can afford to go inside to their reservoir of experience and the myriad lessons they've learned over time, and trust that they can handle anything that comes along. This trust, combined with an expanded self-awareness, makes it much easier to make choices that might have seemed socially risky earlier in life.

Genevieve was one of those women. She was in her mid-sixties when she decided to move to Tuscany. She had been a stay-at-home mom and raised three kids, all of who were successful and happy, and who all seemed to expect her to grow old quietly, like any well-behaved grandmother should. But she had realized just how much of life there was left to experience, and living in Tuscany was high on her list.

"Mom, are you crazy?" her kids howled in disbelief. "You don't know anyone there, and you don't even speak the language. And besides, you're being really selfish. Think of your grandchildren and how they'd feel if you packed up and moved away at your age. It's ridiculous. Why can't you just do volunteer work or something if you're bored? Or maybe you could move into a retirement community if you need a change of scenery." They were adamant—she was not to do anything as rash as moving away, especially to another country. What they hadn't noticed, having taken her for granted for many years, was just what a Bitch she had become. While she loved her children deeply, she was no longer willing to let someone else's opinions, or even their concern, govern her choices. Tuscany it was.

"You know how much I love each of you, and how impressed I am with the kind of people you have become. And I know you want me to happy, just as I want that for you. Living the second half of my life fully is important to me, and I don't want to miss anything that might make my life even richer. So, I'm going to be making some choices you may not agree with, but they are my choices to make. I won't be stupid about it, I love my life too much for that; but I expect you to respect my desire to live a very full second half. Now, I'm starting Italian lessons tomorrow. And when I move, we can stay in touch by e-mail and phone, and you can all come to visit. I've only been to Tuscany once, but I think you'd love it."

This was the gist of her conversation with her kids the day before she began the adventure, as she told me later. They had listened in stunned silence, were still silent when she left to return home, and one of her daughters had called that evening to say that she would miss her, but that it actually sounded exciting. It had been a kind of coming of age for her and for them. She took Italian lessons, and then rented a place in a small town in Tuscany and lived there for most of a year. For Genevieve, the decision to live fully did not originate in despair, or having reached a satiation point in trying to fit others' view of her. Through a daily spiritual practice and a lot of soul-searching, this grandmother of six realized that, for her, part of living as an expression of the Divine was to release her fears and be willing to embrace aspects of life she had never explored.

"Feeling really alive is such a joy. I'm more creative, I'm even more passionate about everything I do," she told me. Her story, like the stories of all true Bitches, reminds me of a piece by Jack London, one of the most important American writers of the early twentieth century who, after a rich and remarkable life, died in 1916:

I would rather be ashes than dust!
I would rather
    That my spark should burn out in a brilliant blaze
    Than it should be stifled by dryrot.
I would rather be a superb meteor;
    Every atom of me in magnificent glow,
    Than a sleepy and permanent planet.
    The proper function of [wo]man is to live, not to exist.
I shall not waste my days in trying to prolong them.
I shall use my time.

So, if the Bitch is a woman who lives full-out and unencumbered by fears that may have limited her earlier in life, does that mean she takes outrageous risks, living on the edge between safety and danger physically, emotionally, and even financially? Absolutely not. The Bitch is not a foolish woman, nor does she have anything to prove by making unwise choices that, on the surface, might make her look bold and daring. Authenticity is the name of the game for the Bitch, and the choices she makes are based on the five elements that support her power: her desire to be of service, her longing to be an expression of the Divine, her self-awareness and self-respect, her way of life that reflects her values and convictions, and her clarity. She has no reason to take up skydiving, for instance, unless she feels a sincere desire to do so without any hidden agendas attached. She has learned to live honestly and openly, and to take on only those pursuits in which she can engage with great sincerity. Does she take risks? Sure, but only those that have purpose for her. And risks come in different shapes and sizes; for one Bitch taking a risk might mean trying something new and challenging, and for another it might mean confronting someone whose behavior is inappropriate. For Genevieve it meant moving to Tuscany, and for Cheryl it meant recognizing her need to be more honest. Bitchhood is not a one-size-fits-all affair.

One does not automatically become a Bitch upon entering midlife. There is a choice involved. It is easier (though sadder and much less rewarding) to choose to see middle age as one of the few remaining pit stops before death, and to respond accordingly. That doesn't take any work, just the willingness to give up, relinquish one's dreams, and live without much to look forward to. Women become Bitches when they have made the other choice at the crossroads that is midlife. So, how does the Bitch become who she is? How does she spin a first half that may have been shaped by fear and the expectations of others into the gold of a fully realized second half of life? And how can you do the same?

It begins with creating a meaningful relationship with yourself. That may sound strange, even silly, so let me explain. I mentioned earlier the importance of falling in love with yourself, and that's what the Bitch has done. Simply living in your own body and going through your day-to-day life does not inevitably result in a relationship with yourself. I have worked with many women who could tell me in great detail what their friends and loved ones feel, think, and want, but who couldn't come up with an answer to the question: What do *you* want? After years spent putting others first (often by necessity as mothers of small children or caregivers for aging parents), women often find it difficult, if not impossible, to identify their own needs. Often, when I ask women what they want, they respond by saying, "I haven't really thought about it." This inability to recognize their desires tells me several things:

- They put themselves on the backburner of life long ago.
- They've bought into the myth that taking care of themselves is selfish.
- They haven't spent time figuring out who they are and what works for them.
- They don't believe they deserve to have what they want.
- They don't know themselves well enough to make choices that work.
- They have neglected themselves in the process of taking care of others.

All of the above add up to women not having effective relationships with themselves. "I don't know what I want, I don't know how I feel, I'm pretty sure I don't deserve love or real happiness, and I'm damn sure I don't know how to make my life something I really want to wake up to." These are the kinds of things that tumble, often unbidden, out of the mouths of women who don't know themselves. How can I make good choices for myself when I don't know me very well? That sad state results in women not getting what they need (which is impossible if they don't know what that is), and ultimately, often at midlife, in feeling empty, restless, unsatisfied, angry, resentful, and even depressed. Who needs it?

Having a loving and nurturing relationship with yourself means feeling at home in your own skin, being able to retreat into your own spirit to get replenished. It means becoming your own best friend.

Think of all the things you do for the people you love, not to get something in return, but simply because you love them. Now imagine what life would be like if you were to begin doing such loving things for yourself. Consider the ways in which life would change if you were your own greatest and most constant source of love.

There is also great responsibility that comes with creating a loving relationship with yourself. You must take action to change thoughts and mind chatter from negative and self-deprecating to supportive and motivating. It requires noticing when the old way of being starts creeping back into your behavior, and respectfully but firmly nipping it in the bud. And perhaps most importantly, you must take responsibility for getting what you need, instead of waiting for someone else to make it happen for you. The Bitch is not a passive woman. Earlier in life she may have spent her energy hoping life would happen the way she wanted; but at this point she has come to understand that if her life is to be what she wants it to be, its up to her to make it so. Often, at midlife, women have come to believe that the possibility of ever having what they need is just a fantasy. After all, if by the midpoint in life it hasn't happened, it's a good bet that it won't, right? Fortunately, it doesn't work that way. In fact, it's at that midpoint that a woman has accumulated what she needs to shape the rest of her life. Everything up to that point it has been, largely, practice.

A big part of developing a relationship with yourself is getting clear about what you need in order to be fully present and open to joy. Once you're clear about that, it's your job to make sure you get it. This can be much simpler than it sounds. You can begin by periodically and randomly checking in with yourself to identify what you're feeling and what you want. The purpose here lies not so much in the response to these questions, but rather in establishing the habit of noticing and acknowledging your feelings and needs. You can't live with passion, joy, love, or peace until you come to understand who you are; that means getting clear about what you think and feel, what you want and need. The Bitch has begun to recognize all this about herself, and gets clearer every day. I say she has *begun* to grasp these things because it's a lifelong process. Every time she respects herself, tells the truth, speaks her mind, and makes choices shaped by integrity, her sense of herself strengthens. Because it's so easy to put yourself on hold while you struggle to meet the expectations of others, it requires intentional behavior to get back on track. This may sound too simple to be helpful, but its power lies in its simplicity. Think about how you form relationships with other people: You spend time learning what they think, how they feel, what they enjoy or fear, and what makes them happy. In the process you have the opportunity to get closer and to form a bond that can grow and deepen over time. But rarely do we do that with ourselves. So, checking for feelings is a way to begin getting to know yourself in a new way. You don't have to do anything with what you find unless you want to, just notice and move on. Every time you do this, it gets a little easier to be aware of what's going on inside.

Approaching this process with curiosity will help you enjoy the experience. Feel whatever you're feeling at any point during your day with no judgment, and no need to change it right away. Just notice, acknowledge—*Boy, am I pissed right now,* for instance—and let it go. Your feelings don't determine who you are, but they contribute to how you choose to live your life. Respect them first, and then if you want, you can change them. As you identify what you want and need at any point in time, you can choose the ones that can be acted on and then take steps to make them happen. Start small: I need to take a break and get some fresh air. Then work up to the bigger wants and needs such as: I need to tell my mother-in-law that it hurts my feelings when she criticizes the way I cook. Some of the things you identify may be more long term, and may require a more detailed action plan and more patience. (Losing weight and feeling better about yourself may take longer than needing to take a walk to clear your head.) You can prioritize according to which are most pressing, most essential to act on. Some will be fleeting; some will be unwise to act on until you know you're thinking clearly. But all are important to recognize.

And every time you let yourself pursue something you want or need, you give yourself the message that who you are and what you want is significant. The Bitch knows that who she is, what she stands for, and what she wants are important.

Many years ago I was on the verge of emotional exhaustion. I was working too much, going to graduate school at night, and raising two children. On top of that, I felt obligated to accept any social invitations from my friends, fearing that if I declined they would be hurt and angry. As I neared a dangerous kind of depletion, I began asking myself what I needed that I wasn't getting. The answer was clear—I needed quiet time for myself, time without obligations or expectations, time (and a way) to replenish the energy required of me on a daily basis. Without it, I would soon be unable to accomplish any of the things important to me; I would end up doing a half-hearted job, hating every minute of it, and probably getting sick.

There was a lot at stake here, the most important of which was my kids. How could I be the kind of mother they deserved if I was so drained I had nothing of value to give? Because my condition was urgent, I knew that urgent measures were necessary. I reduced my work hours, and chose to take only one class the next semester. That would delay completing my graduate degree by one semester or so, but I would still be on my feet and coherent at graduation, which would not have been the case otherwise. And, the most difficult choice of all, I told my friends that I was taking time off in order to get my health and my life in balance. "I care about you so much," I told each one, "and I don't want to lose contact with you. I simply have realized that I am stretched too thin, I've lost sight of my priorities, and I'm headed for some kind of breakdown if I don't change things. I hope you can understand my decision to cut back on social things for a while. I'm your friend, I value you, and I'll be in touch when I'm feeling better." I was scared as I explained this to the people in my circle of friends. What if they thought I was selfish or uninterested in what they needed from me? What if I got my life in place, and then found that, in the process, I had lost all my friends? But when I weighed the options I knew I had no choice.

And then the most miraculous thing happened. I found that, by recognizing and acting on what I needed, I began to breathe again. It was as if I had been holding my breath for years, waiting for the next tough thing that would have to be handled. But now, having honored my need, my breathing was regular, deep, and peaceful. I no longer woke up with palpitations hammering my chest from the inside out, or the vigilance that had come with believing that I had to be responsible for absolutely everything. My children and I once again had valuable time to spend together; and after years of anxiety and the feeling that my life was a tight little box with no room to even blink or swallow, I now had time to notice all the things in my life that had taken a backseat to chaos. There was suddenly beauty all around me, time to appreciate my children, and time to allow Spirit to renew my energy and my joy. Further more, all my friends were still there when, several months later, I re-connected with them. I had learned a valuable lesson about myself: My personality is such that I require time alone to get my energy back after expending it. Some people are wired to get replenished through time spent with lots of people. Others need time apart to get refilled. The Bitch knows which she is, and lives accordingly. Until I took a good look at what I needed, I assumed that I could go on forever being everything to everyone. Now I know better. So I have come to require quiet time for myself on a regular basis. Nothing is allowed to get in the way of that, and as a result I have never again found myself close to the depletion that could have ruined my life. What am I feeling right now? What do I need, and how can I take responsibility for getting it? These are questions the Bitch asks and answers regularly.

Here's an additional way to get clear about what works for you, and what you need to get into a state of power and possibility. Think back to experiences and times of life that were good for you. These might be times when you benefited in some way, or you had feelings that were meaningful, or you were rewarded physically, emotionally, psychologically, spiritually, or financially. Some of them may have happened years ago, and some might be recent. Make a list, and look for two things: What was it that made each experience so good, and what did all the experiences have in common? Write all this down, and then look for patterns.

The second part of this process involves putting yourself into a relaxed state, and then asking your unconscious mind to show you a perfect day. As you imagine this ideal day, take note of the elements that make it perfect. Now, you may find that this ideal day doesn't have much to do with your day-to-day reality; if so, you can do the exercise again, this time letting your unconscious mind reveal to you a perfect day in your current reality. Believe it or not, there will always be elements that can change the shape of your experience and add a touch of the ideal. Those are what we're looking for. Again, once you've allowed this information to surface from your deeper mind, write down what you saw, heard, and felt and find the patterns. Those patterns tell you what elements have consistently made your experience rewarding and significant. Once you've identified them, your happy job is to find ways—some obvious, others subtle—to add those elements to your daily life. The more honest information you have about yourself, the better equipped you are to make changes that open the door to the wonderful world of the joyful Bitch.

We've talked about the actions of the Bitch not being governed by fear. This is essential to her development and well-being. In order to live in this powerful and loving way, you must be able and willing to let go of the concerns and uncertainties that may have shaped the first part of your life. But how to let go of those limiting factors? How to shift from the need to please others and the concern that you may not be able to pull off a truly rewarding life, into that vibrant world of the Bitch? Like any transformation, it doesn't happen overnight—but it can absolutely be done. Your ability to change those things that have kept you from what you want does not depend on anything but your willingness to take an honest and loving look at yourself, and to take on a new and more expansive perspective. If you want it, you can have it.

Fear and insecurity are most powerful when we're in the thick of things, unable to see beyond our concerns. As mentioned earlier, one of the things that allows the Bitch to live so powerfully is her ability to see herself and her circumstances from an elevated view. When she can see the whole picture instead of being limited to what's visible from the trenches, she has a lot more information to work with, and a lot less negative emotion to get tangled in. From that place, she is aware of options she couldn't see from a more limiting viewpoint. I had my first "aha" moment about this several years ago when I was flying to a new city to give a presentation. I remember looking out the plane window as we prepared to land, and noticing how orderly the layout of the city was. From that higher place I could see how the streets were designed to flow into each other, how several streets all led to the same large open plaza, how the highway surrounded the city and provided smaller routes to get to the center of the urban area. I thought to myself that I could find anything, even in this unfamiliar place, if I could look for it from this elevated point of view. It would be much more difficult to find what I was seeking if I had to find it while at street level, without the benefit of that big picture vista. Once in the thick of things, on unfamiliar streets surrounded by unfamiliar buildings, and unable to see how orderly everything really was, I would be lost. Fortunately for me, all I had to do was hail a cab and everything worked out. But the lesson has stuck with me all these years.

The Bitch has learned the value of dissociating herself, usually temporarily, from a situation and looking at it as if she were floating above the set of circumstances, seeing herself and whoever else is involved. She does this as if she were a neutral observer, with no bias or vested interest in the interaction she is observing. From this slightly separate position, she can see the patterns of her own behavior and those of the others involved; and she can do so without having her observations clouded by emotions that can keep her from seeing and understanding the whole picture. That higher perspective lets her see how the situation might be handled differently, and how she can do her part in a way that contributes to the highest and best for everyone. She can then bring that information back into the "thick of things" position and implement the new choices she's perceived from that neutral observer place. As she steps back into the situation, her emotions recur—but they've been molded by what she's learned in that dissociated position.

Another skill the Bitch as developed is to take any Big Picture information that could prove to be overwhelming because of its enormity or complexity (the "I don't even know where to start" syndrome) and break it down into smaller, more manageable pieces. She has learned that she doesn't ever have to take on something in its entirety, and that most things in life are best accomplished small piece by small piece.

Our lives are molded by what we have learned to believe is true. The feelings we have, the choices we make, and the actions we take are determined in great part by how we have learned to perceive life and our place in it. The individual who believes that life is unfair will live very differently than the person who believes that there are opportunities everywhere. In order to become a true and divine Bitch, you must first examine your existing beliefs, identify those that limit you, and then decide what you would prefer to believe, what you as a Bitch would believe instead. Once that's done, it's time speak the old belief out loud, and feel what it brings up. It might leave you feeling sad, angry, anxious, or any number of other feelings, most of which probably don't serve you well. Now, ask yourself, *What if?* What if that old belief isn't true? What if I thought it was true and I took someone else's word for the truth of it, but it actually was never the case. What if I was lulled into believing it was true, but in fact I don't have to even consider it anymore? There is a remarkable rush of freedom that often happens when a woman simply opens herself up to doubting the truth of a limiting belief. *What if?* immediately opens us to the possibility of some alternate belief, one that will move us toward whatever it is we want. This allows us to loosen our grip on what may have been a lifelong and restricting belief. Once that grip has been loosened, all sorts of wonderful things become possible.

Francesca, a homeopath in private practice and single mother of two, came to work with me because she couldn't seem to make enough money to support her family well and put money aside to open a retreat center in the future. "I work hard, I'm good at what I do," she said with obvious frustration, "and my patients tell me that working with me has shifted things for them in many ways. If I'm so good at it, why am I still struggling just to pay the bills?" At forty-three, and with one child ready for college in two years and the other, one year later, she was just getting by. Her plans for the future were big and exciting, but unless things changed financially very soon, none of them would come to fruition.

I asked her to tell me about her relationship with money. "My relationship with it? I don't know what you mean." That told me a lot right away. She had no sense of connecting to money, and "relationship" didn't fit in her financial picture. "Well," I responded, "do you and money have a loving and intimate relationship? Is it a sordid affair you'd rather not tell anyone about? Are you and money estranged, or are you total strangers?" She thought about my question, and finally answered in a very small voice. "I think we're strangers. I feel like I've never connected with money, and certainly never had a relationship with it. It's a complete and scary mystery." The tears started at that point, and I could feel just how confused she was.

"So, tell me what you think is true about money. If you *were* acquainted with it, what would you have found?" I wanted to know what she believed about money that was being reflected in her lack of it. The information I was looking for came pouring out without a moment of hesitation. "Money is out of my reach," she said quickly. "There is never enough money, it's hard to find, you have to sweat blood just to have enough to get by. Only certain people get to have money, and I'm not one of those people. I will never have more than just enough to stay alive. I don't deserve any more than that. No matter how hard I work or how good a person I try to be, I don't get to have enough." By this time she was sobbing, and the pain of a lifetime of lack filled my office. I explained how the unconscious mind was constantly reflecting back to us the beliefs we hold, how our beliefs form a lens through which we see our lives. We draw to ourselves experiences that match the beliefs we carry. Our day-to-day lives are mirrors that reveal to us the ways in which we have limited ourselves. We get to transform our circumstances by transforming our beliefs.

"What if," I asked her to consider, "what if all those things you think are true about money aren't? Take a moment and consider how life will change when you realize that none of it is true, that you somehow took on someone else's ideas about money and now you get to come up with your own." As she thought about this and felt it in her bones, Francesca began to relax. I could see it in her face and then throughout her body—a kind of letting go of a set of beliefs that had kept her a prisoner for years. After all, when we don't believe something is possible, we don't come up with whatever it would take to accomplish it. Negative beliefs keep us stuck in a life that is small and unremarkable. I asked her then to release that old belief to make room for something better. This is a powerful action to take. One of the first things the Bitch has done to opened the door to Bitchhood was drop the beliefs that held her back and replace them with those that could propel her into the life she was intended for.

The next thing I asked Francesca to do was to choose a belief she would prefer. She came up with "There is an unlimited amount of money available to me, and I am open to making lots of it now." I knew this was a good belief for her because of the power she felt when speaking it out loud. She asked herself *what if*, but this time it was What if this new belief is really true? The excitement she felt at this possibility was palpable. I asked her to consider her life from the perspective of there being plenty of money available to her. Everything looked, sounded, and felt different to her when considered this way, and after surveying her life as an opportunity for unlimited abundance, she turned to me and said, "I'm ready." And I knew she was.

Francesca's life and work began to turn around almost immediately after this process. By loosening her death grip on a belief that had kept her hooked on scarcity for years, she had created space in her own heart and mind for abundance of all kinds to flow easily to her. Her old belief had dammed up that flow, creating a self-fulfilling prophecy, and now the dam had broken. Her primary relationship deepened, she relaxed as a parent, and the number of patients seeking her help increased dramatically. The last time we spoke, Francesca had put together a detailed action plan for opening her retreat center. The money and the right people to help had already begun to show up. I asked her how she felt about the changes that were happening. "I never dreamed that I was holding myself back," she said. "I was the only obstacle to my own abundance, and I kept trying to blame it on everyone else, on life, on karma. But it was me, and I was the only one who could change it. Now that I understand that, I feel like I can accomplish whatever I want." What an astonishing way to live a life.

Because she is so focused on taking effective action, the Bitch knows that she must live present in the moment. She is a clear example of what psychologist Abraham Maslow meant when he said, "I can feel guilty about the past, apprehensive about the future, but only in the present can I act. The ability to be in the present moment is a major component of mental wellness." Many, if not most, people—women perhaps more than men—spend the majority of their time either regretting things done or not done in the past, or (often fearfully) anticipating the future, and in the process neglecting the present moment. In reality, the past and the future don't exist; the past is gone, the future has not yet happened, and all we really have is the present moment. As Maslow so wisely said, it is only in the present that we can take action because there is nothing else. If we aren't present in the present, we are wasting our time.

The Bitch thinks differently than other women do. She has developed a mindset that virtually ensures successful action, whether she is a grandmother helping to shape her grandchildren's lives or the head of a multi-million-dollar corporation. She knows that the quality and impact of her life start with how she thinks. There is evidence through history that the great thinkers, the movers and shakers during any period of time, knew that one's way of thinking and perceiving would determine the way one lived. In the Old Testament the statement is made that "As a man thinketh in his heart, so is he."[1] William Shakespeare, hundreds of years later, wrote "There is nothing either good nor bad, but thinking makes it so,"[2] and more recently Earl Nightingale, internationally known expert on success, is quoted as saying "We become what we think about." Man has known (intuitively if not consciously), from the beginning of introspective thought and spiritual exploration, that attitude and point of view set the stage for how one develops. Negative thinkers tend to have lives filled with negative experiences, kind and loving individuals regard life in a way that draws to them experiences touched by love and kindness, and those who look for opportunities tend to find them. What that means, among other things, is that we get to choose the kind of life we live. The Bitch has made a distinct and irrevocable choice. Once she becomes a Bitch, she can't go back to anything less. Once she decides to live as a source of love, compassion, transformation, and action there is no room in her for powerlessness, malice, or whining. And she takes great joy in that.

So, how might we characterize the attitude, the mindset of the Bitch? And how can any woman eager for more joy learn to operate from the Bitch perspective? A list of the elements of her point of view is a good place to start:

- She has asked herself and answered the question, How do I want to live at midlife?

- Once she has answered that question, she has made a firm commitment to living in the way she has identified.

- She has explored the beliefs she's carried through the first half of her life, and has identified and transformed any that have limited her.

- She has examined the meta-outcomes that underlie her stated goals. (A great question to ask and answer is: What is it I really want through achieving this goal?)

- As she is presented with choices and decisions, she evaluates them by determining whether what she is considering will take her closer to or further from both her short and long term goals.

- She practices looking at her life, her goals, her work, and her relationships in Big Picture form, and then breaking each down into smaller, easier to manage pieces in order to avoid overwhelm and frustration, and to move more quickly and effectively toward what she wants.

- She takes some time to search for the deeper meaning in her experiences, rather than simply reacting to a surface interpretation.

- She consistently respects her own feelings, not to the exclusion of the feelings of others, but as equally important.

- She has given herself permission to formulate and express her own opinions.

- She has carefully shaped her values and is unshakably committed to them.

- She has learned to recognize and act on the inner signals that warn her that something needs to be put right.

- She picks her battles, choosing not to waste her physical and psychic energy in skirmishes that aren't an important part of her Big Picture.

And most fundamental to everything,

- She sees herself as a spiritual being; and

- She has fallen in love with herself and with the Divine. (This is not arrogance but true, profound, and humble love.)

These, in combination with the five prongs of her power, make the Bitch a woman to contend with and to learn from.

Many women at midlife have learned to fade into the woodwork of their lives. They have kept their true natures on hold for so long they have lost sight of the vibrance they were born with. They have become flat and vanilla in their attempts to please and to get along. They have watered down their own *joie de vivre,* their vitality, and as a result they seem to be one-dimensional. Life is not meant to be lived that way, and the Bitch is unwilling to compromise and disrespect herself in that manner. Bitch energy is palpable, and it radiates from her. There is often, if not always, the sense in her presence that something dynamic is about to happen. Unlike those who have been lulled into psychic sleep by a toxic level of niceness, she is multidimensional and vibrant. Her life has texture and color, not because of her circumstances but because she has *chosen* to create a life of texture and color.

There's a point that must be clarified before we go on: There's nothing wrong with being nice. And if our only choices were to be either nice or rude, I would certainly opt for nice. However, "nice" rarely shows up in descriptions of or opinions about the Bitch. That's because "nice" is a bland word often used to describe people who have allowed themselves to become so diluted that they don't seem to have any actual personality. During the first half of my life I was disturbingly nice; a relative once told me that she appreciated the fact that I was such a nice girl, and that I never got in the way. "Nice" in that case really meant "easy to control and manage," and it described me to a tee. My toxic level of niceness came from my desperate desire to please others and to be included. I had spent so much time and energy being whatever others thought I should be that I had lost any awareness I may have had of just exactly who I was. It was painful to realize that I had betrayed myself so well and so often that I could easily reflect what others wanted me to be, but without someone else's expectations to rise (or fall) to, I might as well have not existed. I had become a blank slate onto which others could impose their demands, watching as I scrambled to meet them.

While the Bitch is generally given to kindness, compassion, and sensitivity to others, she is not "nice" in that nondescript and featureless way. And, because she has become aware of and willing to express her own feelings, values, and opinions, at some point she is likely to rub someone the wrong way. That's when we get called "bitch" in the street sense, the underlying meaning of which is most often "woman who isn't being what I want her to be," as we saw in my earlier workshop story. The Bitch knows that being called a bitch usually means that she's hit a nerve, that she is requiring excellence and accountability from herself and others, and that it makes those unwilling to commit to that excellence uncomfortable. She remembers to translate "bitch" to "Bitch," and wears the label proudly.

Entering into Bitchhood does not give us license to be rude, hostile, or abusive. Just as being nauseatingly nice to try to get what we want doesn't work, being the woman everyone hates and is afraid of won't either. Remember Delores, the Corporate VP of Terror? Her "my way or the highway" style caused her nothing but trouble. Choosing to live as a Bitch simply means that we have learned how and when to take a firm stance, how and when to state our position on anything, and how and when to make it clear that we will act on our values and the convictions we hold.

Knowing the "when" of all that requires that we know how to recognize our inner signals, those that give us the go ahead on something, and those that warn us that something requires our attention. Everyone was born with an internal system of signals similar to an alarm system you might install in your home. This is intuition. The difficulty is that many people learn early in life to ignore those signals, and wind up getting themselves in trouble as a result. If you put a security system in your home, and the alarm went off in the middle of the night, you wouldn't lie in bed thinking, "There's that damn alarm. I'll just lie here until the battery runs down." You would, instead, recognize that the alarm means there's something you need to handle, and you would get up and carefully address whatever needed your attention. In much the same way, your inner signals are always in place and, when acted upon, can keep you safe and on the right track. You've probably been in numerous situations in which you had to make a choice, you had a strong gut feeling that told you what to do, and the option you chose turned out to be the right one. In those situations you simply knew inside what to do, and the inner signals that pointed you in the right direction then are still available to guide your choices, decisions, and behaviors. I'm sure there have been other situations in which your gut warned you about something, and that warning turned out to be accurate. If you compare those two signals you'll most likely find that they are different, each one designed to give you its own kind of message. These signals aren't arbitrary, they are meant to help you quickly assess your circumstances and make the best possible choice. Most of us learned as kids, however, to regard this unfailingly correct system as an indication that we are being too emotional and illogical in our evaluation. "Ignore those feelings," we are often told as we grow up; "You're being silly; you've got to be more rational." While this admonition usually came from well-meaning parents or other authority figures, its result has been to subtly encourage us to further separate ourselves from the emotions that are a natural part of the richness of our lives.

The Bitch has learned to recognize and act on those inner signals. She knows which feeling means what, and she understands that they never lead her astray. As long as she remains open to them and doesn't clutter her perception with analysis, those gut-level feelings will act as guides to ensure a response that is fitting and resourceful.

So, let's sum up everything that makes this extraordinary woman who she is:

The Bitch may have spent much of the first half of her life feeling self-conscious, unsure of herself, more focused on what others thought than on her own observations. She may have found herself bouncing all over the map as a younger woman, trying to figure out where she fit in terms of pretty much everything. The majority of her precious time and energy were quite possibly spent striving to please others so she could feel better about herself. As a result, during her pre-Bitch years, she may have been on a bit of an emotional roller coaster—she felt good when the people around her treated her well, and like a loser when those same people either treated her badly or were indifferent to her. She had rendered herself powerless in regard to her sense of self by making her emotional well-being and self-esteem contingent upon a particular kind of response from other people. She probably saw and heard things she suspected weren't right or kind or just, but may have brushed off the responsibility for changing those things by saying, "There's nothing I can do. I don't have any power; I have to just make the best of whatever comes along."

And then she had a "hold it" moment, a point in time at which she realized that she was no longer willing to live that way. This life-changing "hold it" experience may have come as the result of a traumatic event or major loss that forced her to re-examine everything, or it may have occurred when she realized that she was simply sick and tired of trying so hard to be what everyone wanted her to be. This most likely happened at about the midpoint of her life; before that she hadn't yet learned to cut through all the constraints and obligations placed on her by others still haunted by their own fears. A remarkable

metamorphosis began as she chose to shape her life according to the
following assertions:

- No, other people aren't better than I am. They're just different.

- No, it isn't okay to treat me in a dismissive way. I matter.

- Yes, as a matter of fact I believe I *do* have an opinion about that
  and here it is.

- You don't have to agree with or understand my opinion, but you
  do have to respect my right to have it.

- My living like a doormat honors no one.

- What I think and feel is as important as what anyone else
  thinks and feels.

- I can tell the truth about what's going on in me and still be kind
  and loving.

- If I don't ask for what I want, I have no right to complain when
  I don't get it.

- I can be an agent of change by living with integrity and
  respect.

- I am a unique creature straight from the hand of God.

- Whatever I focus on in my thoughts, I will get more of. Therefore, I must monitor carefully what's going on in my head.

- There is a gift for me in everything I experience, no matter how
  difficult it may seem.

- I will find whatever I am searching for: If I'm looking for the
  gift, I'll find it; If I'm looking for the pain, I'll find that too.
  Which would I rather focus on?

You can come up with many more beliefs and implement them in
your life. All the assertions and goals of the Bitch are positive, never
vindictive or insensitive. They are shaped by that idea of the highest
and best for everyone involved. They feel appropriate and congruent

when she checks in with that elegant inner system of signals, and she is at peace knowing her intention is clean.

And here is, perhaps, the easiest way to grasp how life is different for the Bitch than for women who have not yet connected with the power they hold. In our younger years, life was pretty much about us. Our focus was on doing and being whatever it took to find our place in the larger fabric of life, and to feel safe and valued. Our first forty or fifty years were, in a sense, preparation for the second half of life, when we would have what we need to manifest the internal power that had lain largely dormant. Becoming this exceptional woman is not inevitable; it is a choice offered to each of us. Upon choosing Bitchhood, the focus shifts from the self toward ways in which to make a difference, enhance quality of life for other living things, and become a channel for healing throughout the planet. The perspective of the Bitch is greatly expanded from what it was earlier in life, and she sees, hears, feels, and responds to life in a profound and inclusive way.

A few simple things you can do to begin calling forth the power of the Bitch:

- Look at yourself in a mirror and say out loud "I love you and I respect you."

Repeat this seven times in a row each morning and evening.

- Do a gratitude exercise every day.

List three different things each day that you are grateful for, you appreciate, or you find beauty in, and write a sentence or two about why each one is on the list.

- Commit to finding one way every day to authentically express who you are.

- Do something loving for yourself at least three times a week.

- Think of something you've wanted to do but haven't, and take definitive action toward the goal.

This can be a class you've wanted to take, a skill you've thought about learning, a book you want to read but haven't, or anything else that feels right.

- If there is a cause you find interesting, explore how you can help.

- Dedicate yourself to a daily practice of self- and Divine awareness.

This may involve meditation, prayer, reading sacred writings, journaling, and even the effective use of powerful affirmations to reprogram old and detrimental beliefs.

- Practice the art of saying "No" when that's what is best for you.

Another great one is "I don't think so," as in "I don't think that will work for me," or "I don't think I like that." Don't do this just for the rush of doing it, and don't use it as an opportunity to throw your weight around. That is not at all the way of the Bitch. The meaningful use of this art will help you feel more real, and help you choose the most fertile places to put your attention and energy. You can follow it with things like "I'm sure we can find a different way that will work for both of us," or "Let's come up with some other choices that fit for everyone." The point is that if "no" is what you need to say in order to honor yourself, then say it. You won't lose those who truly love and respect you. Nobody will abandon you. It will all work out. And every time you respect yourself, you get stronger.

In large part, the task of the first half of life is to define ourselves in relation to a number of groups: What part do I play in my family, my peer group, my community, my church, my country, and so on? At midlife, having done all that, we are free to explore ourselves more deeply, and to define ourselves and our potential contributions in a vaster way. How can I best serve the planet? How can I best honor That Which Is, my spiritual Source? These are the questions that motivate the Bitch. These are different from the questions and concerns that move us as younger women. Having spent our youth addressing the needs of those in our more immediate circles, we can afford to enlarge our vision to include the bigger picture of which the first half of life was a part. That expanded view is summed up nicely in a quote from Virginia Woolf, who said, "As a woman I have no country. As a woman, my country is the whole world."

Eleanor Roosevelt once made a statement that applies most strikingly to women, as they become more aware of the unlimited possibilities available. "Remember, no one can make you feel inferior without your consent." This startled me when I first heard it many years ago. I was struck by the simple truth of it, and the clear implication that each of us has the power to determine how we want to feel. The Bitch, through lots of self-esteem ups and downs, has come to understand that if she is having one of those less-than-powerful days, it's an indication that in some way she has relinquished the internal power that is meant for her alone. Once she realizes that, she can backtrack to the point at which she stepped away from her internal power and re-do things in a more suitable fashion. Sometimes she can take action to actually change the situation and other times, when she doesn't have access to the original circumstance, she can step back into the Bitch state and replay the situation from that point of view. She can also regard the event from the higher and slightly dissociated perspective we talked about earlier. While considering things in this way, she can ask herself questions. What in this situation moved me to relinquish my power? As a Bitch, what could I have said or done differently to remain centered and resourceful, and to create a better outcome? Replaying what happened, this time seeing herself behave with the power and confidence of the Bitch, provides her with a strategy to clean things up quickly instead of digging a deeper hole.

She's an extraordinary woman, this Bitch. She's the one who can be counted on to do what needs to be done, to make sure goals get reached on time and with excellence, and to be a role model for women who want to live exemplary and tremendously productive lives.

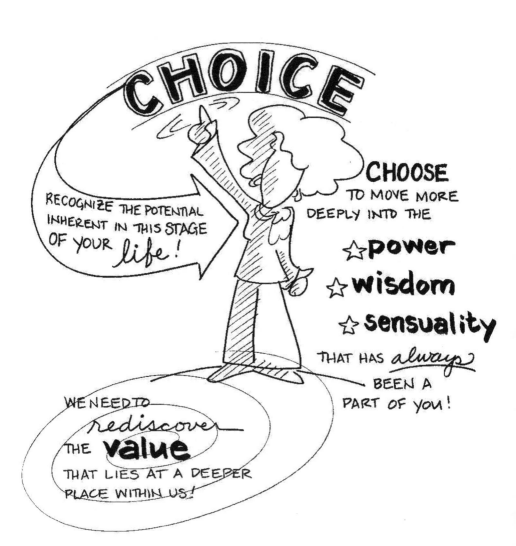

The Crone:
Wisdom and Insight

I recently researched the word "crone" and was surprised to learn that its original meaning was very different from its current definition. The most commonly accepted definition is "withered old woman," a definition based solely, it seems, on the physical. However, in the fourteenth century (the earliest application I could find) "crone" meant "cantankerous or mischievous woman". Such an interesting and disempowering journey we've taken, in the minds of those who create such definitions, from cantankerous (which can also mean feisty) and mischievous to withered and old. Consider the impact of this shift in meaning: Who has more power, the woman who is feisty and mischievous or the one who is old and withered? And which one might be found more threatening?

There is an entire world left out of this "withered old woman" designation—a world that, at midlife, we must explore. In a number of ancient fairy tales, reference is made to the "wise old crone," the older woman whose wisdom, insight, and healing power were sought by younger people who had not yet developed their own. In these stories, people in need went to those who had been alive long enough to find the magical Divine nature within, and generally those were older women. Young men were sought for their physical prowess, and young women for their ornamental quality and child-bearing ability;

but when the need to understand, to intuit, and to heal arose, everyone headed to the wise old crone's place.

Before we can begin to explore the Crone and the splendid world in which she operates, we must define some terms. It wasn't quite as essential to clarify terms when talking about the Bitch, because "power" is defined the same way for both genders, as "the ability to make things happen". So the primary issue we looked at when discussing the Bitch was how that power is used differently by men and women, by the Bitch, and by those women who haven't yet claimed their personal strength. But when we talk about the Crone, we're entering a separate realm.

Wisdom is the quality that characterizes the Crone. On the surface, this seems easy enough to understand, but over time the definition of that quality has become a little mushy and very arbitrary. It's important to understand that "wisdom" and "knowledge" are different. I recently spoke with a young woman who was attending a local university. During our conversation, she mentioned a professor whom she regarded as very wise. I asked her how she could tell he was so wise, and she said, "He just seems to know everything about his field." No, I said to myself, that's not wisdom, that's knowledge. The things he knows about international relations (his field of study) have helped him reach a tenured position at a university, but they won't help him accurately intuit the deeper needs being expressed in any situation, they won't reveal the most effective path to take, and they won't assist him in opening his heart to joy.

We live in a culture in which knowledge is important and highly valued. There's nothing wrong with that. The Crone, however, has taken things to a deeper level. Wisdom and knowledge are not inherently and mutually exclusive, but society, with its primarily external focus, tends to recognize and reward knowledge more readily. Knowledge is gained from external sources: Read informative books, take classes, do research, and you can become knowledgeable.

Wisdom, on the other hand, begins within, and one must be willing to take that daunting journey to the realm of the soul in order to find it.

But how should we understand the nature of wisdom? The Oxford English dictionary defines it as "the capacity of judging rightly in matters relating to life and conduct," a technically accurate but pretty lifeless description of a profound attribute. And then we have several variations on the "wise" theme:

- Wise crack–an insolent or impudent remark

- Wise ass–someone given to insolent or impertinent remarks

- Wise acre–someone who speaks with irritating authority, especially when not truly knowledgeable

- Wise guy–one who is obnoxiously self-assertive and arrogant

All the above appear to refer to wit, pretense, and edginess, and are manifestations of both a superficial attitude and underlying issues. And all take the concept of "wise" and apply to it an edgy and unhealthy energy, perhaps in an attempt—conscious or otherwise—to undermine the power of wisdom and its depth.

For many in the first half of their lives, the whole idea of wisdom is difficult to appreciate. As we've already seen, that early stage in life tends to be centered on taking action designed to establish one's place in the scheme of things. The focus is mostly external, and the need for acceptance and inclusion high. Those who, in their twenties and thirties, are intent on building careers, amassing fortunes, finding love, creating families, changing diapers, and figuring out how to feel better about themselves are not likely to spend time exploring the depths of their own internal wisdom. And, while they may belong to a church, temple, or other religious group, they may not put much energy into examining the teachings themselves, or whether those teachings resonate in their own hearts. The first half of life is all about making things happen personally and professionally, and taking care of day-to-day life. For many at that point, the concept of wisdom feels irrelevant.

There's a reason that those who are considered truly wise are typically older. Earlier in life we have neither the capacity nor the depth of experience required to contain the wisdom that characterizes the Crone. The knowledge that is so valued early in life is held in the brain, and whereas the brain is equipped to hold an extraordinary amount of information, it is not the dwelling place for wisdom. The Crone takes her perspective from a much deeper place, the place we might think of as her essence or perhaps her soul. It is here that she has accumulated a lifetime of experiences and learned to understand them on a deeper level. It is here, also, that she has developed and honed the willingness and ability to perceive all living things as reflections of the Source. Many people, even those who are actively involved in a variety of religious activities, are quite selective regarding whom they choose to love, respect, and treat equitably—in spite of numerous spiritual writings that clearly require love and justice for all. The Crone, however, has chosen to see everyone through the same eyes of love and care. This is a woman whose nurturing and welcoming spirit is offered to anyone she encounters.

At midlife, we have accumulated a body of understanding and insight that allows us to contribute to life very differently than we were able to when we were younger. Whether we realize it or not, we have gathered everything we need to perceive, interpret, and respond at a deeper-than-surface level. In the first part of life, knowledge is more valued than wisdom: We get another degree, develop new skills, and memorize formulas and philosophies—often with self-serving intention. But wisdom and knowledge are different, wisdom coming from a deep place within. In the second part of life, there is a greater emphasis on the internal, and we are able to implement what we have learned in a wiser, more effective way. Our intentions have shifted, our focus is different, and we can see beyond the surface and into the deeper meaning. We can step beyond the limitations of ego and into a much vaster realm of possibility.

I had my first encounter with the Crone when I was a young woman, and I still find the experience comforting. It was a time of life when I ached to be accepted by others, to be liked and to be part of something. I was painfully shy and lonely, and I knew that there were people around me who regarded me as aloof and strange. I was very aware of how people interacted, how they treated one another, and I noticed that in all the cliques that had formed in my community, the only individuals regarded as acceptable and worthy of respect were those who were part of the group. Since I didn't have a group, I wasn't acceptable anywhere. I was left out of everything, and felt like an outsider everywhere I went. The loneliness built over the years, and I became very, very sad. Then, at a local charity organization, I met a woman who was considered both a great humanitarian and an odd and undiscriminating individual, who treated every person she met as if he or she were hugely important.

The people I knew who were given to judging others would talk about this sixtyish woman, Hannah, and roll their eyes in disgust at the way she ministered to the dregs of society as if they were royalty. "I'm sure she means well," one would say while the others nodded, "and I know it's because of her efforts that we have shelters around town and a job training center for the homeless and all that but honestly, have you seen her hug those ... people who come into the shelters? They look like animals—dirty, unshaven, holes in their shoes—and there's Hannah hugging them and acting like she's been waiting to see them. She's probably picked up all sorts of diseases from them. She could get a job working with decent, clean, responsible people; what is wrong with her?"

I remember being intrigued by these remarks, wondering who this Hannah was and why she had chosen to do such work. I thought about visiting the shelter, simply to witness her actions for myself. But I wasn't part of the charity group any more than I was part of the upwardly mobile group, and I didn't feel up to risking any more rejection.

Several months later I attended a conference where Hannah was speaking. The topic was something like "Liberty, Justice, and Respect for All" and she talked to an audience of hundreds about how much society was missing out on by not exploring who the homeless were and what each might be capable of contributing. The audience was made up of social workers, therapists, folks from the department of Social Services, a few from the penal system, and other service areas tasked with tending to those who lived on the street. As Hannah spoke, I heard lots of muttering from those seated around me. "She doesn't know what it's like," and "The best we can hope for is to control and manage them, never mind encouraging them to contribute," and even "Give 'em an inch and they'll take a mile, and probably rip you off in the process." I was fascinated; the very individuals whose job it was to help these people were the ones least inclined to see them with compassion and to recognize the potential in each one. It appeared, to many in the audience, that the people Hannah was talking about and working with were disposable, worth no more than minimal effort. And up on the stage stood one woman, twice as old as many in the audience, whose view of this disadvantaged segment of the population was shaped by the idea that each person was unique and, if given the opportunity, might have something useful to offer.

After Hannah's presentation I thanked her for sharing her experiences. She took both my hands (a gesture that almost brought me to tears), told me how glad she was that I was there, and invited me to visit the shelter to see the work she was doing. I accepted, and was surprised and a little uncomfortable at what I found. I had never seen the inside of a shelter, and had expected squalor and lack. Instead, Hannah's shelter felt like a home—nicely furnished, artwork on the walls, quiet music in the background. During the course of my day there, I saw people who looked beat up, worn out, and filled with despair. But once they entered the place, there was no one who was neglected or left out. Hannah was there to greet each one, and her greeting was like that of a long-lost friend. I marveled at her sincerity with each of these people who, on the street, were almost always ignored or avoided. She shook hands with or hugged everyone, apparently unconcerned about hygiene issues or the possibility of contagious disease. I watched the faces of the guests she greeted, and the impact of her open and kind reception was obvious. People lit up as she made them feel welcome and at home, and I am certain that their respect for her rules was a byproduct of the respect she gave them.

I sat with her for a while at the end of the day, and asked her how and why she was able to live that way. She looked confused for a moment, as if she didn't understand the question. Then a quiet smile spread across her entire face. "These are God's people," she explained. "Each of them was shaped by the hand of the Almighty, each of them has a purpose here, and I see the love of God when I look at them. Their hearts have been broken, they've given up their dreams, and Divine love can change all that. It is my privilege to work with them."

I was amazed. These people were considered the lowest of the low by many, but this woman found joy in working closely with them. Equally surprising to me was the way she welcomed me. With Hannah, I felt important, valuable, and interesting. Her demeanor remained the same no matter whom she was greeting; the least fortunate were welcomed in the same way as those who donated large sums of money to her project.

When Hannah and I first met, her warmth moved through me like lava. I felt as if she could see beyond the things that others had judged me for, and into my core. As I watched her working at the shelter I noticed that she never appeared to judge any of the people who used her services. She gave none of the cold, tight-lipped responses these people got from others, no thinly veiled flickers of disgust, just an unwavering respect for the human experience and its myriad challenges. I saw her bring rough, hostile men to tears simply by hugging them and asking how they were doing. Her place offered more than just four walls and a couple of meals a day; it was with her that these people could find emotional shelter and a bit of the dignity their circumstances had stolen.

The Crone has learned to allow others to be where they are on their individual paths and to understand that, no matter how a person is living, there is a lesson there that he or she is called to learn. That doesn't mean she tolerates inappropriate, unkind, or unjust behavior; she has a fierce sense of justice. However, she knows that the Divine is ministering differently to each of us, and providing every individual with the fitting next step on her unique path. Because she sees everyone as a reflection of the Divine, she respects the path each has taken (as long as it causes no harm to others), knowing that all paths, eventually, lead home. It may take a lot of stumbling and many lifetimes, but they all are designed to bring us back to our Source. How can she judge, knowing this?

I recently met a woman who teaches at one of the toughest high schools in a major metropolitan city. She's fifty-three, average looking, unpretentious, and about as far removed from "cool" as one can be. The school where she teaches has a long history of violence—student-to-student and student-to-teacher. The police visit frequently, and several teachers have been attacked on the grounds as well as in their classrooms.

For most, it's a scary place. But for Jean, it's fertile ground. She's greeted warmly by even the toughest kids, and students who have customized their cars, gotten tattoos, or had their noses pierced seek her out to show off their latest treasures. She has time for everyone, and according to colleagues is the only staff member who never speaks disparagingly of anyone.

"When I was younger," she told me, "I would have felt scared and defensive in this place. I would have taken all these behaviors personally, and would have probably lashed out to protect myself. But I don't feel that way now. When I look at these kids, it's as if I can see into the core of each one and sense what's possible once they learn to channel their energy in a different direction. I ask myself what might be motivating their actions, and I know it's that they're scared, sad, and lonely. How can I feel afraid or hostile toward anyone in such pain?"

Jean chooses consistently to look beyond the behaviors to the soul of each student, to regard each as a spiritual being, and to respond with love, respect, and acceptance based on who each one is, not what each one does. She comes down hard on unacceptable actions, but no one ever doubts her love and respect. For many of these kids, Jean's classroom is the only place where someone cares about and believes in them. And through her exceptional wisdom, she is magically shaping and saving lives.

Throughout history, many cultures restricted the gaining of ancient wisdom to those who had passed through the perilous first half of life and into a place of what we might call "soul sight," the ability to see and understand the soul level aspects of a person, thing, or situation. In the societies more in touch with the earth it has almost always been the elders who were revered enough to be the keepers of the laws, history, myths, and mysteries of the tribe or clan. Shamanic training and practice in ancient cultures was generally restricted to those women who had passed through menopause and, as a result, held their "wise blood" inside instead of losing it during menses.[1] Older women, the crones of a tribe, were the healers, teachers, midwives, and historians, expressing the fulfillment of their experience and the wisdom gained to that point in the life journey.

The Swiss psychologist Carl Jung believed that the purpose of life was the unfolding of one's true Self. He called this process "individuation," a term taken from the Latin word *individuus,* meaning "undivided" or "whole". Individuation, to Jung, is "the process by which individual beings are formed and differentiated; in particular, it is the development of the psychological individual as being distinct from the general, collective psychology."[2] This is an ancient and respected perspective on growth and development through the stages of life; numerous cultures speak of this journey through life and of the process of discovering one's true nature, one's inherent wisdom, and one's profound connection to all of life and its Source.

Jung, whose work was greatly influenced by his own midlife crisis, believed that the task of the second half of life was to maintain and nourish society through, among other things, sharing wisdom gained as we experience the cycles of life. The picture is bigger, the vision expanded, and the circle of our influence potentially more inclusive at midlife. The Crone has passed through the physical beauty and relative innocence of the Maiden into the role of Mother, with its opportunity to conceive and carry new life, and the responsibilities that come with nurturing one's family. She has learned and grown from these roles, and has now transcended them to become Mother to the entire community. In leaving the time of reproduction and the mothering of our own children, we are privileged to enter into the time of life during which we can offer an even greater nurturing, that of both our society and our planet. Brooke Medicine Eagle, in her book *Women of the 14th Moon,* explains this transition as viewed in Native American society:

> When our elders step across the threshold of the Grandmother Lodge, leaving their bleeding behind them, they become the Keepers of the Law. No longer is their attention consumed with the creation and rearing of their own family ... Thus their attention turns to the children of all Our Relations: not just their own children, or the children of their friends, their clan or tribe, but the children of all the hoops: the Two-Leggeds, the Four-Leggeds, the Wingeds, the Finned, the Green-Growing Ones, and all others. Our relationship with this great circle of Life rests ultimately in their hands. They must give away this responsibility by modeling, teaching, and sharing the living of this law—in everyday life—to men, women, children—that all might come into balance.

The Crone has been gifted with an unparalleled capacity for insight and compassion. Since this is the force that shapes her life, she tends to make a fairly natural transition from nurturing her own family or circle of friends to nurturing the community and the planet as her self-concept expands from mother to Mother. In moving away from the earlier responsibilities of raising a family, the Crone is free to apply her Wise Woman qualities, perspective, and skills to a much broader population. Over time, she has become aware of the interconnectedness of all life. She is now able to offer the same compassion and care she has always given to her own loved ones to all forms of life, as family becomes Family, the fabric woven together by the life force, the hand of the Divine.

Compassion is a vital component of the Crone's wisdom—not sympathy, not even empathy, but compassion. This bears examination because, though on the surface they can look similar, with anything less than compassion, the Crone couldn't be the striking woman she is.

There are typically three ways of responding to others as they experience difficulty, misfortune, and even the everyday challenges of life. The response we choose in any situation depends on our relationship to those whose difficulties we observe, the level of responsibility we feel (in general and in a specific circumstance), and the degree to which we become emotionally entangled in the conditions we are witnessing. Sympathy, defined by the *Random House Dictionary* as "a feeling or expression of sorrow for the distress of another," is the "Oh, you poor thing, how awful for you" response that may be followed, silently, with "Thank God it's you and not me." Sympathy can also result in a messy and ineffective entanglement, when it comes from those whose emotions are easily triggered and who are easily drawn into the drama of others. This happens as a result of being thoroughly associated in the situation. When I am so emotionally present in your difficult situation that I can feel your pain and I take it on as if it were my own, that's sympathy. In that state, feeling raw and distressed by circumstances over which I have no control (because they are not my own), I can't take effective action or even make useful suggestions because I am living "under the circumstances". How can I be helpful if I'm feeling as bad as you are? In a state of sympathy, I'm right there in the thick of things emotionally. While I may think that means I'm being supportive, what it really means is that now there are two of us caught up in the drama, and neither of us has the clarity necessary to identify and take appropriate action to change the situation. Remember the paralyzing feelings I had for the people I saw in a devastatingly poor country? That was sympathy; I got so overwhelmed with their despair that I became ineffective. Even if I had been able to take action in that situation, it would have been scattered and unproductive because the emotion I was drowning in had clouded my judgment. Sympathy is akin to pity—though pity, adding insult to injury, tends to regard the one suffering as weak and therefore inferior. Nevertheless, both sympathy and pity feel bad, and neither helps.

In a state of empathy, defined as "identification with and understanding of another's situation, feelings, and motives," we can relate to what someone is experiencing, having been there ourselves, and we can feel like an ally because we know what it's like to be where they are. People who are deeply empathic are able to sense what others are feeling—a gift that can be very useful for those in professions focused on helping. That gift can, however, run amok if not managed well. Empathic individuals must learn how to dissociate emotionally once they've recognized the emotions at work in someone else, in order to protect themselves from sliding into the drama those emotions can evoke. Typically, empathy doesn't involve the wallowing in unhappy feelings that is common to sympathy. Still, it tends to fall short of productive action and does not guarantee kindness or benevolence.

The life of the Crone is characterized by a different gift, that of the third possible response: compassion. In a research paper by Jennifer Goetz, offered by the Center for the Development of Peace and Well-Being in Berkeley, California, compassion is defined as "an emotion we feel when we perceive others in need and want to alleviate that need or suffering." This is not a gushy, hand-holding kind of concern, but rather a soul-level ability to grasp and understand what others are experiencing, and an equally profound desire to relieve unnecessary suffering.

If I see someone who has broken his leg but doesn't know there is help available, I will do everything I can to get him to a hospital so they can set his leg and give him something for pain. It would be unnecessary for him to continue suffering when there are those who can help. But the word "unnecessary" is important here, as there are certain kinds of suffering, usually those that we bring on ourselves, that are entirely necessary in order for us to become everything we are intended to become. For instance, say that I am suffering pangs of guilt because I have stolen money from someone who trusted me. A thoroughly committed do-gooder sees my suffering, wants to make me feel better, and offers to pay the money back herself without disclosing my part in the act. I may accept in order to escape both the shame of being revealed and the need to pay back the money, but I probably will not learn much of anything valuable from the experience. My suffering will have been alleviated, but I will be doomed to repeat the lesson until I finally choose to learn. In this example, the alleviation of my suffering is to my long-term detriment. Had I been allowed to complete the experience in a healthy way (i.e. feeling the guilt until it became overwhelming and I had to confess and make amends for the sake of my emotional well-being), I could have moved on without the emotional, psychological, and spiritual baggage that comes with lessons not learned.

The act of relieving someone of suffering required for growth is most often driven by a personal agenda on the part of the one doing the relieving. This desire to rid the world of suffering, even when in doing so I am assisting individuals to escape responsibility for their own lives, brings relief that is only temporary—both for myself and for those whose (necessary) suffering I am alleviating. The underlying motivation here is often to ensure that, in taking action to overcome someone's necessary suffering, I no longer have to witness that suffering. In that case, my action is pretty self-involved. Let me offer an example: I recently read a story about a meditation group that had been focusing their meditation efforts and discussions on suffering. They all agreed that seeing others suffering made them uncomfortable, and that they wanted to do something to help ease the suffering they had to witness every day on the streets of their city. They took up a collection in order to give money to the homeless individuals living on the street all around them. On the designated day, they agreed to take the collection (about $50) to the street, and to give it away within thirty minutes. Strangely, they found only one homeless man on the street during that thirty-minute period, and wound up giving him the entire $50. Returning to their meditation center, they reveled for a while in how good it felt to relieve suffering.

A couple of days later, they read in the local newspaper about a homeless man who had drunk himself to death after coming into more money than he had seen in some time. It was the man to whom they had given their money. On the surface, their desire to reduce suffering seemed clean, but in truth their intention had been to relieve themselves of the discomfort that witnessing such suffering caused them. In their zeal, they had taken unwise action that led to greater sorrow. That particular homeless man was not equipped to use the money wisely, and it quickly became more of a burden than a gift. This is not compassion. Had they offered to help him get set up with an agency that helps find day labor jobs so he could begin bringing in his own money, that might have been an act of true compassion. The Crone's approach to compassion is, "I can't do it for you, but I will support you in doing it for yourself."

The teen-aged daughter of my good friend screwed up so badly in school that not even the local colleges would accept her and she was faced with getting a minimum wage job that she would hate. Her mother, a Crone in her own right, said "I love you, and nothing will change that. I know you're scared about your future and regretting the behaviors that got you in this situation. You have one year left to get your grades up, and I know you are intelligent enough to make that happen. If you take advantage of this opportunity, I believe you'll be heading off to college this time next year. If not, it will be time to look for a job, and there are lots of fast food places and grocery stores around that are always hiring. It's up to you. I will support whatever choice you make."

Her expression of compassion took the form of offering her daughter options, and allowing her to decide how she wanted to live. She could have forced the kid to study for hours, to prove she had attended school each day, and to offer her homework to be checked; but that would have created even more stress for both of them. The daughter's efforts would have been driven by her mother's dream rather than by a genuine desire on her own part to turn things around and begin creating a life worth waking up to. Or, the mother could have taken over and done the girl's homework herself, knowing that if she did it the kid's grades would improve dramatically and quickly, and college would be a given. Either of those paths would have provided a temporary solution by allowing this very bright girl to continue not to take responsibility for her life and actions. Her suffering was necessary, a push toward a path of accountability.

The concept of compassion is often accompanied by images of tenderness and serenity, and this can create the impression that compassion requires a soft, even passive approach to life. However, nothing could be further from the truth. As H.H. the Dalai Lama has said, "Compassion is not at all weak. It is the strength that arises out of seeing the true nature of suffering in the world. Compassion allows us to bear witness to that suffering, whether it is in ourselves or others, without fear. It allows us to name injustice without hesitation, and to act strongly, with all the skill at our disposal. To develop this mind state of compassion ... is to learn to live, as the Buddha put it, with concern for all living beings, without exception."

In Buddhism, there is great emphasis placed on compassion and kindness, as evidenced by writings from Lama Zopa Rinpoche:

All the peace and happiness of the whole globe,

the peace and happiness of societies,

the peace and happiness of family,

the peace and happiness in the individual person's life

and the peace and happiness of even the animals and so forth,

all depends on having loving kindness toward each other.

Live with compassion

Work with compassion

Die with compassion

Meditate with compassion

When problems come,

Experience them with compassion.

Buddhism is certainly not the only spiritual discipline to emphasize compassion as the only truly effective way of life. Many Buddhist teachings, however, provide perfect examples of the way in which the Crone lives her compassion. For instance, the Buddhist term *bodhicitta* refers to the desire to attain enlightenment for the benefit of *all* sentient beings. You'll notice that it mentions all sentient beings, not just those you already like, love, or approve of. The option of picking and choosing who and what to be compassionate toward is not offered. If compassion is present as an aspect of one's essence, then that compassion is present to everyone and everything alike.

A *bodhisattva* is a being with the bodhicitta motivation, one who desires enlightenment in order to benefit all sentient beings. Buddhist Lama Thubten Yeshe is quoted as having said, "The Bodhisattva sees the crystal nature that exists in each of us, and by recognizing the beauty of our human potential, always has respect. Bodhicitta is not emotional love. By understanding the relative nature of sentient beings and seeing their highest destination, and by developing the willingness to bring all beings to that state of enlightenment, the mind is filled with love born from wisdom, not emotion."[3] This is a wonderful description of the Crone, whose nature reflects the loving compassion that the Buddha referred to when he said: "In the world, hate never dispelled hate. Only love dispels hate. This is the Law, ancient and inexhaustible."[4]

I've met with many people who initially resist the concept of compassion, fearing that it is an indication of weakness. In fact, the opposite is true: Compassion, born of wisdom, is not sloppy or mushy. Unlike sympathy, it doesn't hold the hand of the one suffering and murmur "You poor thing, how awful for you," and it certainly doesn't label anyone "victim" and proceed to treat them accordingly. Compassion sees each being as a carrier of the spark of the Divine, and sees the possibility of enlightenment in each one. Responding from that perspective, compassion is firm yet flexible, soft and consistent, a kind of beacon of love, respect, and acceptance in the midst of the chaos that occurs when ego is running the show.

Now, "soft" doesn't mean powerless or out of shape psychically; "soft" as it relates to compassion refers to the deeper understanding, the clarity, and the drive to kindness that shape the compassionate response. The ego's response to pain, loss, and disappointment generally shows up in one of two ways: ineffective sympathy or a kind of emotional boot camp in which the belief system includes admonitions like: No pain, no gain. If it hurts, it's good for you. Quit whining. What's wrong with you? You'd better shape up. I don't want to hear your excuses ... and so on.

The response formed by compassion, on the other hand, sounds more like: I understand that this is a tough time for you. What do you want in this situation? What needs to change in you, in order for a different result to occur? What one thing can you do right now to begin that process of change? What qualities do you bring that can help ensure a different outcome?

In the same vein, "acceptance" doesn't mean that the one who is compassionate figures that whatever others are doing is fine as is. There's an important difference between "My buddy Fang has killed a few people, he's pretty violent, but that's just his way, and I want to accept him as he is," and requiring that Fang change his behavior while recognizing that he is who he is at this moment and that this moment is the only starting point we have, and responding to him as a fellow Divine spark carrier. Ego tends to hammer others into submission; compassion helps them shape and mold themselves.

Compassion doesn't accept excuses, and does require accountability; it just does it in a way that allows hope instead of flagellation. By consistently and respectfully reminding others of the immense realm of possibility, compassion erodes doubt, fear, anger, and hopelessness. This was expressed beautifully by Lao-Tzu in 600 B.C.E. when he said, "Water is fluid, soft, and yielding. But water will wear away rock, which is rigid and cannot yield. As a rule, whatever is fluid, soft, and yielding will overcome whatever is rigid and hard. This is another paradox: what is soft is strong."[5]

The wisdom of the Crone is not inevitable. The fact that one is old enough to have had a large number and wide range of experiences does not automatically mean that one is wise. The practical, yet almost mystical, wisdom of the Crone is a choice. Each of us carries the capacity for wisdom, but not all choose to recognize and live from that place.

The compassion that is a part of that wisdom is also a choice. The easier choice is to remain focused on ourselves and on how the actions of others are affecting us. This allows us to continue to enjoy the pain/pleasure aspect of partial presence and victimhood. In a perverse sort of way, it feels good to feel bad. When I choose to focus on the things that haven't worked out, the ways in which life has been easier for others than for me, the amount of time and energy I've spent taking care of others, and the ways in which I have been taken advantage of, I can take some pleasure in feeling sorry for myself. For many, the midlife slogan is, "I've been wronged, and it hurts so good." But when I choose to see life through the lens of compassion, everything changes.

The Crone has had as many challenging and painful experiences as anyone else, yet she has chosen to let compassion shape her response to life. So, how does she develop this compassionate perspective? First and most fundamentally, she has come to understand that she carries the spark of the Divine, that she is the daughter of Spirit or God, and that peace, joy, and divine love are her birthright. This is not an arrogant understanding; she is humbled in recognizing her relationship to the Divine. This awareness drives all defensiveness and hostility from her. In realizing that she is loved in an infinite way, she has released any need to guard against real or imagined emotional attacks. That love, from God to self and from self to God, frees her to tap into the deeper awareness, insight, and intuition that allow her to live as an agent of love, compassion, and forgiveness. She has chosen to live as an expression of the Divine in the world.

She also has learned to ask herself a powerful question. Instead of quickly responding to whatever is going on through her ego and pride, the Crone asks herself, "What else might this mean?" This question is designed to reveal alternate meanings for a situation that might, on its surface, seem negative and even offensive. For instance, when faced with someone whose behavior is hostile, the Crone could, in all her humanness, respond in kind. She could decide that the hostile behavior indicates a lack of respect for her, or a threat to her physical or emotional safety. However, in asking herself "What else could this mean?" she might realize that the hostile individual is reacting to some crisis in his or her own life, is feeling powerless and scared, or is basically very unhappy. That awareness, and the time it takes her to explore the possibilities presented by the question, allow her to move quickly into a place from which she focuses on the other person rather than on herself. If I realize that the person who cuts me off in traffic is not necessarily just a self-centered jerk, but rather may be late for something that could change his life, or has just gotten a call indicating that someone he loves has been injured in an accident, or is living with such anxiety that his patience is at a low ebb, I am much better able to bless him and release him, rather than to allow his behavior to affect the way I feel and live. This doesn't mean that I tolerate disrespectful and dangerous actions, or that I live so passively that anyone can do anything and I'll be okay with it. The Crone, like the Bitch, is not a passive individual. As in the Dalai Lama's quote regarding compassion, the Crone witnesses suffering (including her own) without fear, she recognizes and names injustice without hesitation, and she acts strongly with all the resources available to her.

One of the differences between the Crone and others who haven't yet chosen to tap into that reservoir of wisdom is that her responses to the experiences she has are informed by her deeper understanding of what motivates human beings. Much like the Bitch, she looks for the underlying meaning of an action before choosing how to respond. The compassion of the Crone comes also from her willingness to see any situation from a variety of perspectives. "How does life look through *your* eyes?" she quietly asks of everyone with whom she interacts. Her take on things is not the only view, and she knows that seeing things only from her own perspective limits her ability to respond with compassion and power. The experience of the street kid who does whatever it takes to get by may be very different from her own experience, and in order to be truly open to and compassionate toward him she takes the time to grasp a bit of what it's like to live his life.

Think back to the Bitch we talked about who needed to make difficult decisions in her workplace. She did it by imagining deeply what the situation was like for those in management with the responsibilities they held, what it was like for those who had to supervise others, and what it was like for the rank and file whose time and energy were spent in the hands on, down and dirty aspects of the work. As she stepped into each position, she was able to share the experience of those who held them. That information guided her in choosing the best action to take for all involved. The Crone does something similar; however, her efforts to know what someone else is experiencing are focused not so much on selecting action to take, but rather on understanding what motivates an individual or group. She can then find the internal response that is most respectful and potentially most fruitful in that situation. For example, although we can assume that she has no desire to live on the street, she knows that if she is called to interact with someone who does, she can only be effective and helpful if she has a deeper than intellectual understanding of the quality of his or her life. That understanding comes when she asks herself what life would look like if she were living on the street, with no money, no permanent shelter, not enough food, and possibly a great deal of danger? By stepping briefly into what it's like to be that street person, she gains a much deeper grasp of that individual's day-to-day experience and the feelings that come with it. That process allows her to respond with compassion instead of judgment, pity, or even sympathy.

Several years ago I worked with a young man whose drug problem and depression had begun during a difficult childhood. Although his relationship with his parents had improved through the years, he felt bound to his older brother for whom he felt an intense hatred.

"Charlie has always been so mean, so controlling and vicious toward me," he said. "Even when we were kids he treated me like trash, and it's gotten worse since we grew up. Any time I have to see him, I come away feeling worthless, stupid, and angry. I hate the bastard. He's ruined my life. I can stay away from him physically, but I can't seem to get away from these terrible feelings I have for him."

He had tried to talk with his brother about it, but with the brother dismissed him with adamant denial and the clear implication that he was way too emotional, and probably a closet homosexual.

The depression my client was feeling had escalated in the previous couple of years, and he was having trouble holding a job or maintaining a meaningful relationship. His drug use had gotten worse, and he had been busted once for possession. Things didn't look good. As we worked together, it became clear that the confusion and loneliness that resulted from this treatment at the hands of his brother, whom he had idolized as a kid, played a huge part in both the depression and the drug use. His sense of himself had been damaged over time, and he was living like a boat that had gotten loose from the pier and was drifting toward open and dangerous waters.

During one of our sessions, I asked him to pick a place on the floor that could represent himself and his feelings. He then chose a location to represent his brother and all of his feelings. Finally, he selected a point on the floor that symbolized a neutral perspective. Beginning at the place that was his own, I asked him to look in the direction of his brother's spot, and describe his feelings. It was a kind of purging for him, harsh, painful, and honest. I then asked him to shake off his own perspective, and to move into the place that represented his brother. "Step deeply into what it's like to be Charlie," I instructed. "For just a moment, I want you to become Charlie, with everything he deals with, everything that his life is made up of, and then tell me how life looks to you, as Charlie, and how you, as Charlie, are feeling." He hesitated for a moment, briefly unwilling to become this man who had caused so much pain. Then he took a deep breath, and did as I had asked. Almost immediately a shift began to take place. His breathing became rapid and shallow, the tone of his skin began to change, and he tensed up in a noticeable way. "So, Charlie," I began quietly, "I want you to look toward your younger brother standing over there," here I indicated the spot where he had just been, "and tell me what you see, and how you feel." What followed was remarkable. This man, speaking as his detested older brother, revealed the loneliness, jealousy, and self-hatred that had shaped Charlie's behavior since childhood.

"He's always been better, smarter, more attractive than I am. Mom and dad have always loved him more, paid more attention to him. They never punished him like they did me, and they used to tell me that he would make something of himself some day, and that I would probably just limp through life without much direction or success. Everyone doted on him as the younger kid; they all thought he was so cute. I remember when I was five wondering when it would be my turn to get attention and affection from my parents and grandparents. It never happened. Every time I look at him, I remember that I'm nobody, and he's the star."

This was especially notable because I knew that the perceived family "star" had just lost the third job in a row, and had recently been dumped by a woman he had really loved. There was such sorrow in all directions.

I asked my client to shake off the experience of his brother, and return to his own spot. I asked him how what he had just learned about his brother affected the way he felt. "I didn't know," he began, and then started to sob. He had had no idea that Charlie felt so unloved, and so inadequate, and that it was those feelings that were being expressed in the hostile and cruel way he treated his younger brother. "Now I get it," he whispered, as if speaking to the brother he had hated. "I'm so sorry it's been like that for you. I wish I had known sooner." When I asked how he was feeling toward Charlie now, he responded with "I feel so badly for him. I want to help him feel better about himself, and to learn to be happier." That switch from hatred to compassion had taken about seven minutes, and was a direct result of stepping into someone else's experience.

Finally, I asked him to move into the position of a neutral observer, someone who could see the two brothers interacting, but who had no particular interest in what happened between them. As stated earlier, that emotional detachment can bring a clarity that isn't available when strong feelings rule. "Now, from your neutral position, just observing these brothers together, what do you notice?" I asked. His response was practical and very clear. He picked up on things each of them had been doing that had triggered the other, and had suggestions about what he could do to begin healing the relationship from his end. These were observations and suggestions he couldn't possibly have come up with from his own limited and wounded point of view. His new ability and choice to regard his brother with compassion was the beginning of a time of healing and commitment between them. By seeing the world through his brother's eyes, even for a moment, and adding that information to the equation, his response to his brother was changed forever.

The Crone has learned to do the same in all situations. There are several primary reasons why she can live with such compassion for all. First, she knows she is loved by God, and therefore doesn't have to spend energy seeking love from elsewhere. She can instead use her energy to bring that divine love into the world. She also understands that all living things (including Gaia, the earth itself) carry the nature of the Divine within and are, therefore, her kin. And she can step quickly and briefly into the experience of another in order to comprehend a bit of his or her unique path. In doing this, she aligns with White Eagle, who said: "Do not judge by what you see on the surface, but develop an inner vision and insight into spiritual cause and effect. Then you will know that you can judge no man."[6]

Another major and essential component of the Crone's wisdom is her intuition. Defined by the *American Heritage Dictionary* as "The act or faculty of knowing or sensing without the use of rational processes; the power to discern the true nature of a person or situation; insight or instinct," intuition has often been dismissed as emotional fluff by those who pride themselves on their logic. For many, relegating intuition to the realm of things psychic or occult has been an effective way to deny something they don't understand and can't control. There is, however, scientific evidence supporting intuition as a function of the brain. In her book, *The Wisdom of Menopause,* Dr. Christiane

Northrup explains that the gonadotrophin releasing hormones, FSH and LSH, which are actually brain stimulants, elevate at menopause and remain elevated for the rest of a woman's life. As a result, the post-menopausal brain chemistry promotes greater intuition in older women. This, says Dr. Northrup, is the Crone stage, the stage of the wise woman. The elevated releasing hormones offer a physiological explanation of the increase of "psychic" abilities that arise in many older women.

There are additional ways to understand the intuition of the Crone. She has spent her earlier years not only accumulating experience, but also learning to distill that experience in a way that reveals its deeper meaning. Over time and through her transition from external to internal focus, she has developed a longing to know and to honor life, its purpose, and its Source. That longing has moved her from an emphasis on intellect and emotion to being centered at the level of the soul. From that untainted place deep in her own essence, the Crone knows things her intellect and her conscious mind cannot know. The Crone knows what she knows.

For the sake of clarification, I want to emphasize the fact that this shift of focus from external to internal is not an act of self-centeredness. The Crone hasn't quit being concerned for others in favor of focusing on her own needs. The shift instead moves her away from needing approval and validation from others and toward a deep, unshakable knowing, as well as an awareness of her own spiritual nature and her relationship to the Divine. From that place of deep inner knowing, her relationship to the external world is expanded and enriched. And from that place she draws to herself people, things, and experiences that are appropriate for her at that time. It is also in living from that place of inner knowing that the Crone can put her wisdom and insights to their best and most effective use. By being focused on the richness of her inner world, she can be a true conduit of peace, power, love, and wisdom in her outer world.

Some Crones have been inclined toward the intuitive, right-brain approach to life since birth, and have found it to become enhanced and more focused at midlife; but other Crones lived the first half of life with logic at the helm. I rarely meet women who are so immersed in the left-brain, linear way of perceiving and interpreting things that they have completely neglected the more creative, intuitive, and relational aspect of themselves. As women, it's tough to live comfortably while denying those things that are so natural to us. But many women who spend much of their early lives in business settings, for example, are encouraged to ramp up their logical, linear thinking capacities in order to maximize productivity and remain competitive. For these women, approaching problems, challenges, and life in general from a logical and in-control perspective becomes a way to survive and hopefully to thrive professionally.

Many of us also grew up in family situations in which emotion, an emphasis on relationships, and anything outside the realm of logic were discouraged. "You're too emotional," we were told. "You're not making sense. You're too sensitive. You're not being practical." And then there's my favorite, "Geez, you're so emotional; it must be that time of the month." Accusations such as these are all thinly veiled indictments of the sensitivity, empathy, compassion, intuition, and ability to form meaningful connections that are inherent in us. Just as with many professional women, a large number of women raised in such environments learned early that working hard to develop the left-brain capacity for logic was a way to survive emotionally and psychologically.

The (real or imagined) control that comes with a logical approach allows us to feel safe in places where we might otherwise get chewed up and spit out. The difficulty is that, when used exclusively, such an approach leaves little or no room for expressing the qualities that are natural to us as females. And any time we actively seek to repress our true identity, we automatically ensure that our inherent gifts can't be accessed, our capacity for achieving excellence is compromised, and our sense of who we are and what we are capable of is diminished.

The Crone lives fully present in the power of her own gifts, rather than trying to mold her actions and attitudes to someone else's vision. This doesn't mean that she isolates herself, insisting on her own way in everything. That would not be Crone behavior. Whether she is taking action on her own or at the request of someone else, the Crone has learned to use her gifts with impeccability to reach the intended outcome.

Janice came to see me because she had been trying to build a home-based business for about a year, and so far her lack of success had been spectacular. Her business involved products to make the home safer, and the company manufacturing these products had an excellent reputation. Janice was a warm, kind, and loving woman with a genuine concern for the well-being of others. Her initial commitment to the business and its underlying concept had been strong, and she had started out eager to help people live safer, healthier lives.

The man who had gotten Janice involved in the business was male to an excess, focused on getting information and then taking action, a little aggressive, and less interested in the lives of his potential customers than in the statistics that demonstrated the quality of his products. He had been in the business himself for several years, and had been very successful. He had shown her graphs indicating how many people she needed to talk to in order to sell enough to make money, and he had given her a notebook filled with clever ways to respond to common objections. "You've got to take the bull by the horns," he had told her at the outset. "It's all about the numbers. To be successful, you've got to set appointments with a lot of people, and show them how much danger they're in by using other products. Tell them about how many diseases are linked to products that aren't as safe as ours are. Warn them that they are putting their kids in danger if they don't use our products. You've got to scare them to save them."

Janice had tried for a year to do business in the aggressive and logical manner he had presented. After all, she reasoned, he was so successful; his way must be the best way. And since she had never done anything like this, his way was all she had to go by. But nothing had worked. Her presentations to potential customers had felt stiff and unnatural, and she was uncomfortable using fear as a motivator. "Maybe I'm just not suited to it," she told me in our first visit. "Maybe I'm not tough enough to be successful. I guess I should give it up and get a job. But I'm so disappointed. I know these products are important. Why can't I help other people understand that?" Her commitment to helping improve peoples' lives was clear, and so was the solution to her dilemma.

"Janice," I asked, "what would you have done if, when you began your business, you had just been told to help people understand the importance of using such safe products? How would you have done it, if it had been left up to you?" She had spent a year of her life trying to be someone else, and denying the power she carried. Taking someone else's word for how to accomplish a goal without making allowances for her own inherent talent, her own special style, had resulted in nothing but discouragement and frustration.

"Well," she said quickly in response to my question, "I would invite people, women mostly, to my home for coffee and I would just tell them that I had found these products, and that they are more effective, safer, and less expensive than the products I used to use. I might mention the diseases that harmful chemicals are linked to, but I wouldn't show all the charts and tell all the terrible stories about children dying from exposure to the chemicals. I think I would just focus on how much they love their kids, and want them to be safe and healthy." This strategy was brilliant because it was honest and natural to her. Her intuitive approach, had she trusted it, would have allowed her to reach her goals in a comfortable and natural manner. In denying her own intuition and style, she made the road to success much more painful than it needed to be.

Another possible source for intuition, especially at midlife, is the collective unconscious, a psychological concept conceived of by Carl Jung. While working in the area of psychic phenomenon, he found indications that human psyches were actually linked together in both subtle and profound ways. He termed this shared body of wisdom and knowledge, as well as the profound connection among human beings throughout time, the collective unconscious. The term refers to that part of a person's unconscious which is common to all people, and which contains archetypes or symbols that are understood by all cultures. In other words, the collective unconscious holds the wisdom of the entire human species. All the ideas and philosophies, every thought ever held in the minds of humanity, all are contained within this storehouse, as are all the spiritual and mythological symbols and experiences common to human beings. Because of the timelessness of the contents, Jung felt that these archetypes are inherited from age to age, and have existed throughout all of time. What this means is that the experiences and feelings I have now have been had by others in different times and places, and we are connected by these common experiences and understandings. So then, when we are operating intuitively, are we tapping into a collection of wisdom as old as time itself, and yet consistently current? And if so, who are we to dispute that wisdom?

The Crone readily taps into that ancient and abiding reservoir of wisdom through her focus on the Source of that wisdom. By choosing to live as a conduit of the love and wisdom of the Divine, she has opened a pathway, a direct route to the enduring perceptions of the ages.

And that brings us to the most profound understanding of intuition, especially as it appears at midlife. The women who choose, at the midpoint of their lives, to move into the power and wisdom of the Crone are able to do so because they have aligned themselves with their spiritual Source. Over the course of their lives these women, many of whom may seem quite average on the surface, have moved closer and closer to a re-merging with that from which they emerged. Like drops of water rolling back to the ocean which is their home, every experience of the Crone's life, every lesson learned, every joy, and every grief have brought her nearer to the full recognition of her own spiritual nature. The closer she comes to living and breathing that divine spark she carries, the better access she has to the mind of God and the wisdom therein. When you can tap into that endless resource, intuition becomes a way of life—even Albert Einstein, whom we often consider a prime example of logical, scientific thought, said, "I want to know God's thoughts; the rest are details."

This notion of return, however, is only a metaphor, as none of us is ever really separate from Source. It's easy to buy into the illusion of separateness in the course of a life filled with the challenges that are part of being human. But in truth, we are spiritual creatures having a human experience, and our true nature is always present within— whether we are aware of it or not. The Crone has spent the first half of her life remembering who she really is. She spends the second half living it.

Intuition functions on the physical, emotional, mental, and spiritual levels, and each of us experiences it differently. On the physical level, the body is the vehicle and may alert us to an intuitive insight through tingling in the skin, a knot in the stomach, a feeling of lightness, or some other signal. Mental images, an inexplicable attraction or aversion to a stranger, a sense of connection to God, a gut feeling or hunch ... these are only a few of the ways in which intuition can manifest. The Crone has learned, often through trial and error, that it's wise to trust her intuition; it won't lead her astray. Ignoring or second-guessing it is an open invitation to disappointment, pain, and even danger.

Many years ago I met a man to whom I was very attracted. He was good-looking, creative, our humor was similar, and he found me intriguing. "Wow," I thought one evening after only our second conversation, "What a combination. Maybe he's the one." At that moment, I heard the words "Don't mess with this one; he's a child." The words were so clear that I looked around to see who was speaking. There was no one there, only my sexy new friend walking away from my door, toward his car. "What?" I asked silently, hoping I had misunderstood. Again I heard the same message, even clearer this time. "Don't mess with this one; he's a child." This had to be Spirit, I figured, and I must be in some kind of danger for the warning to be presented so dramatically. But, I argued, he's so intelligent, so sweet, so respectful ... How could he be dangerous? Maybe I misunderstood. No, there it was again a third time, and even louder. I was clearly being warned, but I was already blinded by this beautiful man. Okay, I said to Spirit, I don't understand and you may be overreacting, but I won't mess with him. I'll just ... have coffee with him occasionally. Maybe dinner now and then. That's all. Really.

Two years later, after a long parade of deceptions, betrayals, and only the illusion of intimacy, I realized, through a fog of immense pain, that if I had honored my intuition that evening on my porch, I could have avoided all that pain. All I had to do was remember that the Divine is not whimsical, and does not guide us in directions that are unhealthy or devastating for us. This is not a cruel God who enjoys our pain. There is purpose to everything that issues forth from the sacred realm and I am called to trust that, whether or not I understand or agree with it. Had I simply taken the direction I was handed two years earlier, I would not have had such wounds to recover from. A friend of mine refers to this as "two-by-four therapy". She says that the intuitive messages tend to start quietly, and if we hear and respond quickly, the situation doesn't have to escalate. When, however, we choose to ignore the message, Spirit has to gradually increase the volume until we listen. That increase in volume often brings with it an increase in pain.

Today I pay better attention, and am more likely to pick up on such guidance and act on it quickly. I still make mistakes, still have to clean up messes I could have avoided, but I listen differently now. I am better equipped to hear between the words, to notice the subtle clues I didn't recognize when I was younger. I have chosen to trust both the Divine and myself.

Everyone carries intuition within, but many people never use it with intention. They may experience it once in a while, the "Oh, wow, I *knew* she was going to say that" sort of thing, but however, has put energy into the strengthening of this gift in order to become more effective in don't take steps to develop it any further than the occasional flash of awareness. The Crone, everything she does. There are a number of ways to increase the flow of intuition, and to become more aware of the information and wisdom that can lead to better choices, more joy, and a richer life. Shakti Gawain, whose work with visualization and intuition has been helpful to individuals around the world, mentioned in an interview with Dr. Jeffrey Mishlove of the Intuition Network that learning to relax the body in order to get in touch with oneself at a deeper level is essential. She went on to say that the most effective way to increase one's intuition is to ask the simple questions:

- How do I really feel right now?
- What do I really want?
- If I trusted myself in this moment, what would I do or say?
- When I put aside any mind chatter I may be hearing, what do I know is true right here, right now?

Since we tend to spend a lot of time in our heads, while intuition so often comes through the body, she suggests dropping consciousness down into the area of the solar plexus, as if that were the center of awareness. From there, it's easier to find that "gut feeling".

The Crone has built a collection of ways to access her intuitive wisdom, beginning with relaxation of both body and mind through diet, exercise, yoga, tai chi, meditation, prayer, or other means of releasing both physical and emotional tension. She has refined her awareness of her body's responses to people, situations, and information. She knows that her body is always giving her information through its responses, and if she is paying attention, that information can guide her wisely and save her a lot of emotional, physical, and psychic wear and tear.

Think about it—we're talking about the ability to tap into the wisdom of the ages and, even more fundamentally, the wisdom of the Divine. There can't be anything more powerful, more comforting, or more efficient than that. Yet, we so often dismiss, ignore, and distrust the information provided by this always correct, never-lead-you-astray tool. Why are we so willing to disrespect such a reliable guide?

The answer lies, I believe, in our relationship to ourselves. The Crone, in her pre-Crone days, struggled with this as much as anyone might. Second guessing her hunches, dismissing her insights as indications that she was being too emotional, muting her own inner voice in favor of the popular opinion, the young Crone-in-training was often torn between her own internal experience, and the expectations of others. Reluctant to appear weird to those she might hope to connect with on some level, she may frequently have watered down her impressions and intuitive flashes, and attempted to be ordinary. But this gift won't be denied for long. Eventually the task of hiding her intuition likely became much tougher than flowing with what was natural to her. It is at that point, upon recognizing the lush inner world available, that women at the midpoint of their lives often choose to step fully and deeply into the rich and textured realm of the Crone.

But, let's get back to the question posed earlier: Why do we tend, especially during the first half of our lives, to deny and ignore our own intuitive information? When we are younger and still pretty concerned with how we are perceived and received by others, our focus is external. We look to those around us for an external sense of ourselves and our value. If we're caught up in questioning our own basic acceptability, we are much more likely to seek validation from other people rather than from our own internal awareness.

The external focus so common during the first half of life leads many (if not most) women to trust others more than they trust themselves. As we develop the habit of turning to sources outside ourselves for answers, we neglect the development of our own inner resources. Now, add to that the struggle with self-esteem that most of us experience while growing up, and the messages with which we are bombarded from childhood on about our place as females, and it becomes even more difficult to trust information and impressions that come from within.

If I have learned that: Other people know more and better than I do; I am too emotional and sensitive; I have no power except when it comes to household matters; I am an ornament; I can only exert influence while and because I am young, physically attractive, and a possible sex partner; my value is negligible except in relation to others whom I serve; my ideas and feelings are often silly and illogical ... then it's unlikely that I will be able to take my gut feelings and intuitive flashes seriously. I will probably notice and quickly disregard them because I know that if they came from me, they don't count.

I recently spoke with a woman who told me that her strategy for life was to do the opposite of whatever she was thinking of doing. "That way, I can't go wrong," she said, rather proudly. "I know my own ideas are usually pretty stupid, so if I just do the opposite I'll be making the right choice." Holy moly, I thought, this woman's soul must be starving! Her whole life has been spent disrespecting herself and figuring that everyone else on the planet knows better. And what wonderful gifts are the rest of us missing out on because she has chosen to ignore who she is and what she could bring to life?

It is abusive to regard oneself with such disrespect. The Crone has moved through this stage of self-neglect and abuse, and has formed a profound and intimate relationship with herself. She has been able to do this, in part, because she has gotten clear about what's true for her. She has owned up to who she is at this point in her life; she's identified and acknowledged her strengths and weaknesses, her passions, fears, and joys; and she's not hiding anything. There's huge freedom in that. She can simply *be* without having to prove, hide, or pretend anything. She has, in a sense, become her own deepest and dearest friend and source of support. Each of us is given the choice between honoring and disrespecting ourselves. Because the Crone has chosen to be honest about herself, and to treat herself with great love and respect, she now understands that the impressions and intuitive insights that occur to her can be trusted and honored.

Through the process of gaining clarity about herself and about the Divine within her, the Crone has cleared an internal pathway straight to the still, small voice that never misleads. This reminds me of a time, several years ago, when I was in a challenging personal situation involving several other people. One day I was pacing back and forth on my deck, weighing all the factors and possible ramifications in this difficult circumstance. There were various voices in my head, and the noise was painful. "If I do *this*," I said to myself, "then so-and-so might do *that*. But then this other person could react in *this* way, and that might result in this other kind of horrible thing. Maybe I should ..." The din in my mind was deafening, and I felt like I was being sucked deeper and deeper into the drama. Suddenly, an image appeared to me of a pile of trash with something of great value lying at the bottom. Obviously, the only way to get to the treasure was to work my way through the trash, getting rid of it layer by layer. All of a sudden I understood: The pile of trash was the drama, and all the scenarios I had been entertaining in my head. As long as I kept them alive by revisiting each possibility and re-experiencing the emotions connected to each one, I was just re-arranging the trash. To get to the truth about the situation and uncover the inspired solution, I would have to get rid of the trash. I spent the next hour acknowledging each possibility, and dismissing it. They were, after all, only possibilities. As I neared the treasure at the bottom of the pile, I felt as if I had purged myself of the chaos, and was cleaned out and ready to uncover the best solution for everyone involved. When I suddenly heard/felt the answer, it was like opening a beautifully wrapped and carefully hidden gift. It came as a quiet voice from somewhere deep within, and a feeling, equally deep, as if everything in me was saying "Ahhhhhh, there it is. That's right." Great comfort, great peace. At that moment, there was no more "What if?" or "But if this, then that," kind of chaos in me, just a knowing. I was clear. I knew what needed to be done, and I knew how to do it. That knowing brought with it a feeling of completion, even though there was still work to be done. On some much deeper level, in simply uncovering the solution, I had already addressed the problem.

This is such a fitting example of the importance of the Crone getting out of her head and back into a place from which she can tap into so much more than just her logic. Many, perhaps most, maybe even all Crones have spent time and energy in their younger days striving to be logical, and to do what they *think* is right rather than what they *feel* is right. They may have worked overtime to silence that still, small voice so that they wouldn't come across as too emotional, and so that they would have a better chance of being taken seriously. In the course of all that striving they had experiences that, in retrospect, they knew would have been different had they just listened to what was going on intuitively. They also watched other people taking pride in being thoroughly logical, missing clues pointing in other directions, and cutting themselves off from an entire realm of success, meaning, and joy.

After half a life of this, those women who choose to step into the domain of the Crone know better than to ignore such inspired guidance. To do so would be like having access to a guide who could take her safely and successfully through unfamiliar terrain, but insisting on ignoring his guidance, doing it her own way, and falling into every abyss and predator's lair along the way. There is a lot of unnecessary pain and complication when things are done that way. It is much easier and so much more enjoyable to allow the guide, who knows the terrain intimately, to escort her while keeping her safe. This is how intuition works, as a guide through the sometimes precarious and confusing terrain of the human experience.

As the Crone has expanded beyond just logic, she has remembered how to read her body's responses as vehicles of intuitive information. She sees, hears, feels, tastes, and smells the insights presented to her, and her body provides unmistakable signals when her intuition is active. This doesn't mean that intuition by itself will provide all the information she needs to address life's challenges and live well. Jonas Salk, M.D., developer of the Salk vaccine for polio, was a proponent of the use of intuition in partnership with logic in order to find the most complete information about anything. He is quoted as having said that the intuitive mind tells the thinking mind where to look next. This is the alliance among the mind, the body, and the spirit that the Crone has developed and is constantly refining. The more she loves and trusts herself, the more evident her intuitive power becomes. The clearer the connection between logic and intuition, the more effectively she uses the two together. Many Crones begin this process of accessing intuition with a question that's simple to ask, but not necessarily easy to answer: If I really loved and respected myself, what would I say or do right now, in this situation? By stepping into what it feels like to love and respect herself, the Crone finds easy access to the information and insight that may have eluded her early in life when she had learned to dismiss her own wisdom.

The other part of what moves women to ignore those bursts of intuitive wisdom lies in our understanding of the spiritual realm, gained most often through religion. It is important to note that I am differentiating here between spirituality and religion; when I refer to religion, I am speaking of a set of tenets developed and presented by someone else, to which the individual is expected to mold and adjust herself. In other words, religion is external to us, and we are expected to take it in and adjust ourselves around it internally. Spirituality, on the other hand, begins within as an internal and individual experience of the Divine, and radiates outward into the world. Taken further, spirituality is the expression of our own spiritual nature as we go about the business of living our lives.

If we have learned that God is so darn righteous and such a perfectionist that the rest of us really annoy Him in our obvious lack of righteousness and perfection; if we have learned that He is an angry and punishing God, a real taskmaster; even if we have learned that ours is a loving God who will send us directly into eternal suffering if we don't accept and follow the "right" teachings, rules, and regulations ... then we are quite liable to refuse and deny our intuition, because (1) We can't be recipients of special wisdom and insight because we're no good and certainly not worthy, and (2) God is already irritated with us because we're no good and unworthy, and so certainly wouldn't waste perfectly good bits of intuitive awareness on us. Lives lived from this perspective tend to be based on fear, and fear prevents us from recognizing our intuition and realizing our place in the heart of the Divine—and it certainly keeps us from creating lives filled with love, joy, and abundance.

Fear is, of course, the opposite of trust, so any time the Crone finds herself sliding into fear, she asks "What have I done that has taken me away from trust and into fear, and who am I not trusting?" Recognizing the way in which she moves out of trust and into fear allows her to be more aware of it the next time, and to correct her course more quickly. The trust, love, and joy are constant, always available; in order not to experience them, we have to move away from their source. I am reminded of a story I heard a long time ago. A young couple, newlyweds, enjoyed taking long rides in their truck, which had bench seats. When they were first married, the young wife used to sit right next to her husband as he drove, rubbing his neck and running her fingers through his hair. These were times that always felt close to both of them. As the years went on, she moved farther from him, little by little, until one day, after ten years of marriage, they were driving in the country, the wife sitting right up next to the passenger door, and she said "Sweetheart, what's happened to us? We used to sit so close when we went for our drives. Now look at us. What's happened?" Her husband, eyes on the road ahead, responded, "I haven't moved."

Trust requires familiarity with and, ideally, an intimate experience of that which one seeks to trust. You probably don't tend to trust strangers; how could you, without enough information to know whether or not they are trustworthy? However, once you take the time to become familiar, you can decide whether trust is appropriate. This is one of the reasons why it's so important to begin developing a profound sense of who you really are, separate from your professional role, or even the role you play with your family and loved ones.

Exploring the gifts you brought into life (without any "yeah, but" stuff), noticing the qualities you carry that are important, giving yourself credit for the worthwhile things you've done, even paying attention to the things you appreciate about yourself physically ... All these help begin to build the trust in yourself that is part of the basis for intuition. If, in this process, you begin hearing things from the past that didn't serve you well then, and sure don't serve you now ("You'll never amount to anything; you're not that smart, you're just not the kind of person who'll ever be successful" and so on), you can identify whose voice it is you're hearing, picture that person, and respectfully send the negative messages back where they belong. You see, most of the negative things we learn to believe about ourselves have come from someone else, not from within us. We just got fooled into thinking that the unfortunate opinions and attitudes of others were true, and so we bought into them. The very good news is that you can send those ideas back where they came from, and go on without them. That makes travel into an excellent future much lighter. Imagine this: Maybe when you were a kid your mother spent a lot of time explaining that "You're a woman, and women don't need to be successful. You just need to find a man and get married, that's all. And besides that, it's much harder for women to be successful, and after all you aren't the smartest girl around. You need to be thankful for whatever comes your way, and don't try to be something you aren't." Now, here you are, in the process of starting a new business, and every time you feel tired, frustrated, or a bit overwhelmed by what's involved you hear your mother's voice reminding you that you probably don't have what it takes and you'll probably fail. These repeated messages begin to wear you down, and to erode the excitement you had felt about your new venture. "Maybe she was right," you say to yourself; "Maybe I should give it up and do something easier."

In this situation, you have a couple of options: You can allow your mother's pessimism to determine your level of success, or you can recognize her message for what it is, her own limiting perspective, and gently send it back. Wisely, you choose the latter option. With an image of your mother in your mind, you say to her lovingly, "Hi, mom. I know you said all those negative things about my ability to be successful because you love me and want to protect me from disappointment, but I'm moving forward with my business now, and those messages don't help. So, since they are your perspective, not mine, I'm giving them back to you. They really don't belong to me, after all; they've always been yours. I just got confused for a while and thought that maybe they were mine. But now I'm clear that they belong to you. So, here they are and I hope you enjoy them." With this, you return them to the image of your mother, and allow yourself to feel the sense of completion it brings. Now, you might be thinking that you'd rather actually meet with your mother, say what you need to say, and tell her that you're giving back the ideas she shared so long ago that have continued to hold you back. And you can do that, if it seems important—but you should be ready for protest and an increase in drama as she defends herself and her point of view. Generally speaking, there's no need for all that. It is usually quite sufficient to use the process detailed above to release both your mother and her ideas. That doesn't mean you don't love her, but rather that you realize that you and she are different, and that each of you is entitled to the viewpoint and lifestyle that feels most appropriate. Neither of you, however, gets to impose yours on the other. You can explain and demonstrate, but not impose. That leaves you free to live as you choose to, while allowing her the limitations that feel comfortable and familiar to her. Without those old ideas weighing you down, you can get a much more accurate sense of yourself, and move more quickly and completely into a high degree of trust in yourself, your choices, and your intuitive impressions. These are the makings of a real Crone. You know how to trust your true friends; it's probably time to become your own truest friend.

For many women, learning to love and trust themselves is much easier than learning to trust a God they have been trained to understand as menacing and vengeful. But the truth about God is found inside: in the depth of joy that comes with our experience of loving and being loved; with the discovery of beauty where we don't expect it; with our awareness of the life force pulsing throughout the natural world; with those peak experiences in which, even if for only a moment, everything seems exactly as it should be. These and other such times are the palest of clues to the nature of the Divine, and our place as Its creation. When we choose to be aware of these things, our capacity to love and trust that which we cannot see is reawakened, and our inner channels, through which love and wisdom are meant to flow, get blown clean.

Our ability to trust Spirit is enhanced through time spent in meditation, prayer, and contemplation. To be strengthened and deepened so that trust is possible, any relationship requires the same degree of intimate experience and familiarity. Falling in love with God is less likely if our understanding of Him/Her/It is theoretical and based on someone else's concept. It is in time spent in our own experience of the sacred realm that love and trust can develop.

Numerous teachers who specialize in the study and application of intuition, including both Shakti Gawain and Marcia Emery, Ph.D., adjunct professor at Aquinas College in Michigan, have stated categorically that intuition is one hundred percent correct, and can be trusted one hundred percent of the time. While I concur, my own experience having been that intuition, as an aspect of the self, doesn't lead us astray, I have spoken with many individuals who assure me that they have followed their intuition and found it to be wrong. My only response to this argument is that if we are not paying attention, it's easy to think we're being intuitive when in truth our perceptions and actions are being motivated by something much less clean than our intuitive instincts always are. For example, remember the man I spent two years with, even though I heard the words "Don't mess with this one; he's a child" when we first met? I found it fairly easy to discount that voice by saying to myself "He and I must be meant to be together, because we have things in common, and we usually enjoy each other's company. If it weren't right to be with him, I wouldn't want time together so much. I feel too connected to him for it to be wrong." Now, was that my intuition, or desire, neediness, and maybe just a touch of lust? Had I stepped out of the emotion for a moment and looked at the relationship from an elevated and objective position, I am certain I would have known immediately that my drive to be with him was not based on any intuitive understanding, and that I was probably in jeopardy if I moved forward with it. In that situation, I didn't explore that deeply; I didn't want to know.

It is essential that the Crone learn to discriminate between her intuition and the myriad other voices that can lead her in less productive directions. Before taking action, she asks herself an important question: Is this my intuitive wisdom speaking, or is this the voice of fear/desire/need? The more she exercises her intuition, the stronger it becomes and the better she gets at recognizing it and not being fooled by cleverly disguised imitations. And the better she gets at recognizing and acting on her intuition, the more effortless it seems. When the Crone is living in alignment with her purpose and her Source, acting out intuitive guidance feels very natural, a way of life that flows easily. Typically, when we are experiencing true intuitive insights, they are accompanied by a sense of peace, an increase in energy, and even a feeling of aliveness. Any feelings of anxiety, neediness, or inappropriate urgency are likely indications that the information being received is not coming from the Divine and the reservoir of ageless wisdom, and should be examined carefully before action is taken.

Now, there's nothing wrong with wanting something, and a bit of lust now and then doesn't hurt, as long as it's channeled in an appropriate direction. But let's call things as they really are. If I want to buy a sexy little sports car because I think it will be very cool, and I get a thrill when I think about driving it, and I choose to interpret that thrill as intuitive evidence that I am intended to have that car, I may be fooling myself simply to justify the purchase. Maybe not, but I owe it to myself to check with as much objectivity as I can find before entering into such a transaction. If it's my intuition providing the thrill, then I can assume that it's the right thing to do, and the price (financial and psychological) that will be exacted won't be a problem. If, on the other hand, I hear from my intuition that I should keep my distance from a man who is a very poor choice for a partner, and I put my hands over my ears and begin singing "La, la, la, I can't hear you," I should be prepared for the price I will be required to pay—and it will probably be a painful one. A true Crone has come to distinguish between the signals that indicate intuition, and those that are based on emotion. She honors both, but in different ways. And she never uses the gift of intuition to rationalize choices and actions she knows in her heart are motivated by emotion, rather than higher wisdom.

I once worked with a couple having trouble in their marriage, and the pain between them was palpable. During the course of their eleven years together, and between the births of their two children, he had had several affairs, and she had become dangerously depressed. For a couple of months, I worked with each of them individually and the two of them together every week. He vacillated between defensiveness and terrible shame, and whatever had moved him to behave in such a hurtful way was deep enough that I knew it could take a while before he would even recognize his part in things and choose to change. And even with months of work, he might still choose to blame her and escape accountability. She, on the other hand, had accepted 150% of the blame for his actions. Her self-esteem was non-existent, any hopefulness she might have had had been pounded into oblivion, and she could only see herself as the bad guy in the situation.

"I know this is all my fault," she told me between sobs. "If I were a better person, more attractive, more interesting, he wouldn't need other women. Can you help me change?" I asked her what else his behavior might mean, but she could only focus on what he had convinced her were her failings. It was a very sad situation, between two lonely and insecure people with issues that had haunted each of them for a lifetime. I knew that dealing with those issues would take time, and I wasn't sure she could hang on much longer in the face of such unrelenting depression. In one of our individual sessions, I asked her to go inside and find the answer to "What can I do to take better care of myself?" but all she found was the certainty that she had no choice but to stay in the loveless and destructive relationship. I knew that wasn't her only option, but I also knew that she had to be the one to discover other possibilities. For several sessions we worked exclusively on the accessing of her intuition. I knew it was possible that she would choose to stay despite the emotional danger, but I wanted to be sure she was equipped to locate that inner wisdom in order to make a decision. She worked hard, and within just a few weeks she was finding her inner voice regularly.

In what turned out to be our final couple's session, we began with his litany of the things she had done the week before to irritate him and drive him to other women. Suddenly, as he paused to take a breath, she spoke in a firm voice. "You're scared," she said quietly. I turned quickly in surprise; this was so unlike her, and I was concerned that she was heading over the edge. But she looked calm, almost serene as she continued to speak. "You're afraid that if you make a real commitment, you'll be so vulnerable that I will be able to hurt you really deeply. Running around on me is your way of protecting yourself. But, you see, what you've done instead is to push away the one woman who has loved you for years. I don't think it will change, and I don't want to live this way any longer." With that, she stood up, thanked me for my help, and left. After a moment of silence, he stood, told me that the whole thing was "a load of crap," and walked out, slamming the door. I sat there for a moment, marveling at what had happened. What she serious? Did she mean it? Would she come back?

I heard from her several days later. She had hired an attorney, was filing for divorce, and had already begun looking for a place for herself and her children to live. We met for a final appointment, and I asked what had sparked her response in our couple's meeting. "It was the intuition work we've been doing," she stated. "As I worked on finding my inner wisdom, I got clearer about what was really happening between my husband and me. And suddenly, in the session, I felt his fear and all the pain that went into it. For a split second I felt that I should stay and help him find a way out from under all that, but then I knew that he wasn't yet willing to do that, and it's not my job to fix him. I have to take care of myself and my kids, and that means leaving my marriage."

Wow, I marveled, what an extraordinary transformation, and in such a short period of time. If she and I had just worked with her intellectual or even her emotional understanding of her husband's condition and the patterns in their relationship, it would have taken months and she would still have felt obligated to stay in the hope that he could and would change. By getting in touch with her intuitive wisdom, the clarity was immediate and untainted by guilt or fear, and the energy necessary to take action became available. She was on her way to a new life, a direct path to her own Crone-ness.

A life without the benefit of intuitive awareness is a life only partially lived; without the advantage of this reliable guidance, we are in for a lot of poor decisions, unfortunate mistakes, dead ends, and unnecessary pain. Through all the struggles and screw-ups that were part of her earlier life, the pre-Crone gathered bits of experience and understanding that began to weave together in a rich tapestry, revealing the consistent love, power, and wisdom of her Source. Now at midlife, knowing as she does that she is adored by the Divine, and that her wellbeing is central to the mind of God, the Crone is careful never to disregard such divinely inspired direction. She's far too wise to refuse guidance that makes life easier, and her path clearer. For those who, throughout time, have chosen to become true Crones, intuition is a portal to a life of richness, peace, and meaning, and a path to the mind of God.

For the Crone, one of the byproducts of being connected to all living things is a vast curiosity, and her desire to know all she can about everything with which she is interrelated serves as another aspect of her profound wisdom. It's not that she's interested in taking up glass blowing, or snowboarding, or learning to speak Chinese; but she wants to know what those experiences are like for those who do them. "Why did you decide to do that? How did you learn? What does it feel like? What do you like about it?" are questions she asks about all sorts of things. Understanding that she is spiritual kin to everything that carries the life force, she is interested in knowing how life looks, sounds, and feels from all those different perspectives. By broadening her own horizon through a constant process of learning, the Crone becomes increasingly effective in the use of her wisdom and its various aspects. It is as if she is saying to everything around her, "We are connected; help me understand and learn from you."

This ongoing curiosity and wonder about life not only ensures a lifetime of learning, but also means that the Crone is never bored. Boredom occurs when we have quit exploring ourselves, our world, and life in general. The reality is that we need never run out of things to learn and to find intriguing, or at least interesting, if we express our natural curiosity. The Crone lives with what William James called "metaphysical wonder," a kind of awe that permeates all her experiences. This being the case, she doesn't dismiss certain people or experiences as unimportant, but rather sees in everything and everyone some reflection of the Divine. Rather than spending her precious time and energy judging those whose choices may not align with her own, she seeks to understand and relate through the web of life that connects her to them. Once she has found that understanding, there is no need to judge, whether or not she agrees; rather, she blesses and releases those whose path is different.

Of course, as I pointed out earlier, there are certain things she won't tolerate—unkindness, injustice, abuse, deception—but she has become wise enough through her own process to realize that each path is different, and each holds the lessons unique to the individual. She expresses her willingness to trust Spirit to lead each person in the direction intended, and holds to the maxim, "Be who you need to be to learn what you need to learn." By understanding why you are, for instance, aggressive and competitive when I am neither, I can allow you to walk that path and learn the lessons associated without feeling the need to change you or to be changed by you. I don't have to agree, but I can grasp the basis of your way of life, and let you go.

I've worked with several couples whose relationships were failing, and who blamed the demise of love on boredom. "There's nothing new to experience; I know everything about my partner, and I'm bored." This is a classic example of what I mentioned before—the failure to continue exploring. There is no end to things to discover about oneself, each other, and how life works, but we must be committed to the exploration. If you are bored, then you have quit exploring, and you may be living from what in Zen is called Expert Mind. This is an attitude in which there is no room for new information because the individual believes she's learned all there is to learn in a particular area. Writer Merry Browne has said it well: "Preconceived notions are the locks on the door to wisdom." The true Crone, however, spends her life in Beginner's Mind, a state of awe and openness to the mystery surrounding her. Everywhere she goes, in everything she does, she knows there is so much more to learn, to experience, and to appreciate.

Keep in mind that knowledge is human, wisdom divine. That being the case, the Crone may not be the person everyone goes to for answers to their technological problems or their marketing issues. We have help desks and consultants for that kind of information. And that kind of information changes quickly and often, as our intellectual understanding and our skill grow. Writer Sandra Carey is quoted as saying "Never mistake knowledge for wisdom. One helps you make a living, the other helps you make a life." The wisdom of the Crone, on the other hand, is sought and applied to the emotional, psychological, and spiritual challenges that have been a part of the human experience since the beginning of time. Her insights have a much deeper foundation and source, and apply today just as they applied as humans first began establishing themselves on the earth. Because the nature of Source doesn't change, our nature as Its creation has remained the same since the beginning of time. Our circumstances have changed, our technological sophistication has grown, we know more about creating things than ever before; and, just like our ancient ancestors, we still love, fear, doubt, defend, seek to possess, and wage war. The state of the human heart is much as it has always been, and therefore the wisdom of the Crone has been applicable throughout the course of time. The Crone doesn't need recognition as an expert in the realm of the intellect; she takes joy in simply living as a vehicle for that which goes far beyond anything the human mind can conceive.

Living as a Crone requires trust in oneself and in the Divine. It requires an ongoing and ever deepening relationship with both—and that takes work that can be periodically uncomfortable. Because of the work involved, and the probability that change will also be required, there are numerous Crone "wanna bes" in the world who seek the title without earning it. You can pick them out of a crowd because their walk doesn't necessarily match their talk. These are those individuals who think that if they dress exotically, pepper their conversation with New Age lingo, and loudly proclaim their psychic gifts, they are automatically in touch with that deeper realm and are therefore members of the sacred circle of Crones. If it were that easy and required that little of us, wouldn't there be a great deal more wisdom in the world than there is? Those who seek instant Crone-hood may be able to present the appearance, but certainly not the substance of those whose lives have been spent learning to access the deeper realms and gaining the compassion, intuition, insight, and love that are criteria for Crone-hood.

The good news is that each of us carries the seed of the Crone within us, and we can each choose to develop into this extraordinary woman as the cycle of life brings us to its midpoint and beyond. By asking for the gift of seeing through the eyes of God, loving that which we might at first think unlovable, offering compassion that goes beyond our human capacity, looking for the meaning that lies deeper than the surface words and actions, and seeking the wisdom of the ages and the mind of the Divine, we begin the process of transformation. This is a sacred and life-long process, taking us moment by moment nearer to the Source from which we have come.

In her book *Gifts of the Soul,* Laura Hyde makes a statement that applies throughout life, and that the Crone has come to understand in a profound way; "No one will ever honor us more than we honor ourselves," she says, and that bit of wisdom resonates clearly. People will always take their cue from us as to how we should be perceived, received, and treated. Those who have learned to love themselves, and to live from a place of great self-respect, and resulting respect for others, will be treated with respect by those with whom they come in contact. Those who doubt their own value, who are confused about where meaning and purpose lie for them, will be treated as if their value is, indeed, in question.

Ms. Hyde goes on to say that midlife is a powerful time, a time when we may long to strengthen the connection with the soul. She tells us that it is a period of looking inward, taking stock of our lives, and releasing that which no longer serves or is no longer valuable in order to create space for that which has deeper meaning.

So, here is our Crone: compassionate, highly intuitive, head-over-heels in love with the Divine, and nurturing of herself. She is accepting of others' struggle to find and follow their paths, always curious and filled with awe and wonder about even the simplest things, and inclined to live a deeper life than those whose experience is more like a stone skipped across a pond—touching the surface on occasion, but never exploring the depths.

But there is something else that has cleared a path leading her directly to the profound and eternal wisdom of the ages. The Crone lives in a state of perpetual forgiveness. One of the lessons she's learned over time is that negative emotion—anger, resentment, fear, sorrow, bitterness, defensiveness—masks wisdom. Although each of us carries the capacity for this infinite wisdom, if we are also holding on to any emotion that doesn't align with the lightness of the Divine, those negative feelings mute and mask that capacity like a wet woolen blanket, heavy and uncomfortable. Another way to think about it is to see that holding onto negativity is like dragging a trunk full of bricks everywhere you go. It's heavy, difficult, and slows you down, and there's no point as these aren't bricks you can use to build anything useful. But we get used to all that pain and difficulty, and after a while it begins to feel natural, as if life is intended to be so arduous. Until we realize that it's okay to let go and move on without the bricks, we tend to keep them very close as part of who we think we are.

Negative emotion operates like tar in the body: dark, heavy, thick, and very slow moving. Because wisdom is light (not dark, and not heavy), it can be overshadowed by the presence of these dark and heavy feelings and the attitudes that keep them alive. No matter how justified a negative emotional response may be, the Crone has learned, often through painful early-life lessons, that each negative feeling, when clung to, serves as a brick. With each new layer of negativity, these bricks become a wall that separates her from her joy and from her Source. Although earlier in life it may have, in some perverse way, felt good to crawl off into a corner to lick her wounds and feel sorry for herself, she has come to value joy and possibility more than pain and victimhood. Instead of erecting a wall that separates, the Crone has chosen to forgive quickly whenever the need arises. Just as is the case with love, when we choose to move fully into our profound identity as spiritual beings reflecting the nature of the Divine, we don't get the luxury of picking and choosing who we will forgive. The true Crone (and all beings who recognize the impact of who they really are) does not love or forgive selectively.

Forgiveness is a way of being, not a feeling. It is also a choice. Forgiveness is not the same as approving of what someone else has done; it is an act of freeing oneself from the painful bond created by the lack of forgiveness. I've worked with numerous people who resist the idea of forgiving because they think it's a sign of weakness, or because they believe that in forgiving they are approving and accepting whatever painful thing has been perpetrated. "I'll think about forgiving him or her as soon as I feel like forgiving," is often the declaration I hear when I suggest that forgiveness is an integral part of the healing process. What's left out of this idea of forgiveness as a feeling, however, is that as long as we hang on to and don't forgive whatever we're angry, defensive, or in pain about, the "feeling" of forgiveness can't occur. In order to let the past go and create space for a meaningful and loving present and future, we have to first choose to forgive.

In order to begin the process, start paying attention to where you are focusing your attention. Do you find yourself periodically drifting back into past situations and replaying conversations, considering all those witty and cutting things you *should* have said and taking great pleasure in the stinging impact of your snappy comeback? Do you find it somehow satisfying to think about the ways in which other people have hurt or taken advantage of you? Do you secretly enjoy it when people point out how unfair others have been to you? Are you still beating yourself up for mistakes you've made, even though they may have happened years ago? If you answer "yes" to any of these questions, or if you have to think about it for a while, it's a good bet that choosing to forgive yourself and others will free you from the burden of the past, and assist you in turning around to face a potentially rewarding future.

Remember what we said earlier: You will get more of whatever you focus on, dwell on, or think about often. When you hang on to old, negative situations and take pleasure is replaying them and re-experiencing the difficult emotions involved, it means you're stuck in that emotional place—and that moving forward into something more rewarding will be difficult if not entirely impossible.

The Crone doesn't hold grudges, nor does she hang on to old sorrows. She can't afford to let her attention and energy get scattered by living with one foot in the present and the other one in the past. Nor can she afford to split her attention between regrets about the past and apprehension about the future. Just as is the case with the Bitch, the Crone can only live with the richness that is intended for her if she is fully present. The Crone can only access her wisdom in the present; that wisdom is meaningless if she tries to apply it to the past or the future, because neither exists. The past is over, and the future is something we can only imagine. The present is all we have, and it's only in her profound experience of the present moment that the wisdom of the Crone has impact.

Living fully present requires that we forgive so that we can release the past. Lack of forgiveness creates a bond, a kind of umbilical cord between ourselves and whoever we haven't forgiven, and as long as that bond is in place the other person has great power in our lives. Think about it like this: Until we forgive, the wound in us stays raw and the pain is always there. We may not be constantly aware of that pain, but an unbidden memory or a thoughtless comment can trigger the pain we thought we were over ... and suddenly we're right back where we were when the unforgiven event first occurred. What that means is that the person we haven't forgiven still has the power to govern how we feel. If someone has betrayed me and I'm still hurt and angry, and if seeing that person intensifies those feelings, that person is, in a very real sense, in charge of how I feel. Once I have chosen to forgive, however, the act of forgiving disarms the past. Neither the person who has hurt me nor my memories of the betrayal have the power to generate unhappy and unresourceful feelings in me any longer. That, in turn, means that I can now channel my energy and emotion in the direction that serves me, rather than being at the mercy of something from the past. When I forgive, I become more powerful and much wiser.

Contrary to popular belief, forgiveness is not for the benefit of the person being forgiven; it is, instead, a choice that frees up the one doing the forgiving. Think back to that umbilical cord between you and someone you haven't yet forgiven. That bond that connects you is made of all those negative and painful emotions you've been hanging on to, the anger, grief, sorrow, and defensiveness that keep the past alive in your mind and in your heart. The choice not to forgive is also a choice to maintain the pain, and that means staying stuck in a past you can't change.

Deep wisdom and a high quality of life require full presence, which in turn requires that all baggage from the past be resolved and released. Resolving the past sometimes involves honest communication with the one to be forgiven, and the mutual decision to be done with past difficulties between you. But, what if that kind of communication isn't possible? What if the one I need to forgive is gone, or has died, or won't respond to my desire for resolution? Does that mean I have to stay stuck? Absolutely not.

As pointed out, forgiveness is for you, not the person you forgive. Generally, the person you release won't even be aware of your choice to forgive, and wouldn't understand or even care if he or she were aware. That being the case, if your intent is truly to let go of the past and move into a meaningful present and future without the weight of unresolved issues, you really don't need the other person's participation to do it. Often the desire to have one final conversation in order to forgive is really a desire to say all those things we wish we had said at the time, and to have some kind of self-righteous impact on someone who has caused us pain. This is not Crone-like behavior. Real forgiveness is clean in its intention to recognize and internalize the valuable lessons inherent in a painful experience, and then to wrap up the past and move forward without the pain. Inflicting pain as a parting shot isn't part of the deal.

The Crone doesn't get bogged down in life's circumstances because she has learned to forgive quickly and to avoid erecting the barriers between herself and others that happen when forgiveness isn't present. This leaves her in a state of emotional and spiritual lightness, and in that state she is much less vulnerable to the heavy and dark emotions that keep others stuck. That lightness allows her to rise above any circumstance, and to find the gift in whatever is happening to and around her. Mark Twain, who carried a good amount of Crone energy himself, expressed the power of forgiveness in a most remarkable and insightful way when he said, "Forgiveness is the fragrance the violet shares with the heel that crushes it."

There are several ways to continue the process of forgiveness, and you may come up with others as you explore this path that leads to emotional freedom. As you experiment with any or all of the following, you may find that one works especially well for you in all situations, or that certain tactics are effective in some circumstances, while other situations require a different approach. These suggestions are just the start of the process of forgiving. As you use them to transform the way you think about and interpret life's difficult situations, you will find it easier to let go in a clean way and start over.

- Ask yourself: What might have moved this person to do this to me?

- After your initial response (which may still be tinged with pain), ask yourself: What else might have been going on in his or her life to result in this?

- Imagine that you have floated to a point above the painful situation, and that you are observing yourself and the other person from that slightly removed vantage point. Pay attention to what you notice as you watch, without being so emotionally engaged in what happened. From that place, you'll see things about yourself and him or her that can help change the way you feel.

- Try something we talked about before: Describe the situation from your own perspective, then move to a different spot in the room where you can step into the other person's point of view, and try describing the difficult event from his or her perspective. This requires that you be willing to take a few minutes to "become" the other person, to take on his or her feelings, to imagine what life is like for that person, and to recognize whatever motivated his or her actions. Finally, move to a third position in the room where you can become a neutral observer who is watching the situation from a completely objective and unattached state of mind. When you've finished, move back to your own spot and take in what you've learned from the insights of the other person, and of the neutral observer. How do those insights affect your earlier painful feelings? How do you feel about that other individual now that you have a better understanding of how things look and feel to him or her? What did you learn about yourself and the other person from seeing things as a neutral bystander? What can you do right now to begin letting go of the past?

The woman at midlife who chooses to discover her wisdom and become the Crone has moved into a different realm, the realm of Spirit. She knows that when she is in Spirit, she has a different kind of knowing about herself, others, life, and the Divine. With this profound knowing, we can transform and heal ourselves and our planet.

There is a Hopi prophecy that states that "When the Grandmothers speak, the earth will be healed." It is the Crone who is the vessel for this healing.

"we must live what we know"

living through my SENSES

I am in rhythm with THE EARTH, WITH THE ELEMENTS, THE BEAUTY IN NATURE and with THE SPIRITUAL KINSHIP AMONG living things

I respond to the world around me with *energy* and *grace*

REFINING our natural SENSUALITY

I HAVE COMFORT IN *my own soul* !

beauty

joy

wonder

physical pleasure

THE HARLOT

3

The Harlot:
Awareness and Passion

The Harlot may be the most intimidating of the three archetypes of a successful middle age because she represents the most personal and intimate experience of this exceptional time of life. Symbolizing more than just sexuality at midlife, the Harlot speaks to us about the power of the senses, and the deeply personal responses—sometimes but not exclusively sexual—that the experience of our senses can evoke.

Ancient harlots lived by their senses, and their survival depended on their ability to stimulate the senses of others. In many cultures, women expected to provide sexual services were carefully trained in the art of pleasure. While I don't endorse meaningless and indiscriminate sexual behavior, there is something important about sensuality to be learned from these women who were often despised in public and desired in private. Harlots were openly committed to the pleasures of the senses and, in order to do their job well, worked to refine their own sensuality and their artfulness. I believe we, too, must explore and refine our natural sensuality if we want lives that are filled with beauty, joy, and wonder as well as physical pleasure. Women of all ages are sensuous creatures, and our sensual nature demands our attention.

Rarely do I find the words "sensuous" and "middle-aged" in the same sentence. One of the myths that convince women to give in and give up at midlife is that sensuality is the privilege of the young and that, after a certain age and particular biological changes, we are no longer sensuous. But sensuality has nothing to do with one's hormone levels; rather, it is a product of the choice to live in a very present state, very much aware of one's senses. Sensuous women of any age see, hear, feel, taste, and smell their lives in vibrant style.

Celia is the most sensuous woman I know. We've been friends for years, and I continue to marvel at her sensory awareness, and at how joyfully present she is in her every experience. Celia isn't gorgeous in the popular sense; her five-foot-two-inch frame is softer and rounder than fashion magazines would consider attractive, and her face is pleasant but almost plain. She wears her long red hair pulled back during the day, but once the sun goes down she shakes her hair loose (even when she's spending the evening at home with friends) and lets it cascade down her back in thick waves. This ritual seems to announce that with the onset of evening comes the promise of something rich, sensual, and even exotic. When I first met Celia, I thought this hair thing was just part of her seduction strategy, designed to put men at her mercy. Now, however, I know better. It is, instead, the fulfillment of an agreement she must have made in another realm before entering this life—the agreement to be a demonstration and a reminder of the endless richness available to us in every moment.

Unlike many other, mostly younger women I have known, whose sensual and overtly sexual moves were intended to seduce and to gain them attention, Celia's behavior is up front and honest, with no hidden agendas and no self-serving intention. This is a woman thoroughly in love with life. She has faced as many tough situations as the rest of us—a painful divorce, the death of one of her children, a frustrating medical condition that sometimes slows down her body but not her spirit—but none of it has dampened her anticipation of joy. And Celia is as sexually active as anyone can be without passing into an orgasm-induced coma. And she's sixty-one years old.

Men have always vigorously pursued Celia, and middle-age hasn't changed that. It's her awareness, her presence that draws them. As I mentioned, she doesn't have the fashion model body, and she hasn't taken any strenuous action to fight off middle-age spread, but it doesn't seem to matter. Her warmth, eagerness to know what other people are about, and openness to adventure draw experience to her like a magnet. She still finds sex intriguing, but now for different reasons. We recently spent a weekend together in the company of several other women, a sort of casual women's retreat. During a conversation about sex, a couple of the women mentioned that they had pretty much lost the drive that had made sex an important part of their relationships earlier in life. "It's menopause, you know. There's nothing I can do about it. I'm not interested in sex any more, and I wish my husband would just leave me alone." Others commented that the sexual aspect of their marriages or relationships had been a superficial element, and that they had moved beyond that need to deeper things. As I listened, I watched Celia's face. This woman, who so blissfully inhabits her own sexuality, seemed to find the conversation confusing. "But wait," she interrupted at one point, "What about giving pleasure to another person, to the person you're committed to? How can you lose interest in that?" What ensued was a brief discussion about whether men who are sometimes annoying deserve pleasure, and then Celia began to share her view of sex at the midpoint of life and beyond. It was a discussion none of us would ever forget.

"Of course, sex is different now than when I was younger," she began. "And I can honestly say it's better. It's not just about orgasm anymore, although I'm certainly in favor of orgasm. Sex has a much deeper meaning now, and a deeper reward. I simply love it, and part of what I love is that when I enter into it in an appropriate frame of mind, sex is really fun. When I'm making love, every inch of me feels alive; I transcend the mundane things of life, I go somewhere else.

It's a spiritual experience, and a light-hearted one. It can be intense, but not heavy, meaningful but not ponderous. When my desire is to connect with another person, and to use my sexuality to nurture, comfort, and give pleasure, it becomes something wonderful that I benefit from, too. I deserve the pleasure, and the men I choose to be with deserve the nurturing and the comfort. I can see the value of it on a man's face as I touch him. There's joy in being taken care of sexually. Now, parts of my body aren't as sensitive as they used to be, and sometimes arousal takes a little longer and orgasms may not be as thunderous as they once were. But you know what? My brain is the greatest sex organ I have, and as long as I'm regarding physical intimacy as an extraordinary gift I intend to have sex until I'm too old and weak to welcome a man I love in that way."

There was a group gasp at that last sentence, the allusion to sex as a special kind of welcome. At that point the ice was broken, and the remainder of our conversation was pretty juicy. I found it remarkable that as several of our friends were rolling their eyes at the thought of their partners' sexual overtures, Celia was silently issuing an invitation—"Bring it on, big boy"—and they did.

I must clarify something here before we go on: There is nothing cheap or trashy about the Harlot, or my friend Celia who embodies the archetype so well. The Harlot, at her best, is a woman with an elegant spirit, a woman who is selective and discriminating about where and with whom she has her sexual encounters, and a woman who has learned to take great joy in using every aspect of herself (and her Self) to express the power of connection. Part of her unique wisdom lies in her understanding of the body as a conduit for all kinds of wonderful and significant things.

Our discussion about sex and the middle-aged woman ended with Celia sharing several techniques she found useful, and a story I won't go into here that involved chocolate syrup, whipped cream, one very ripe strawberry, and about forty-five minutes of mind (and body) bending stimulation. "My eyes were crossed by the time it was over," she laughed as the rest of us sat in reverent silence. A couple of weeks later I ran into one of the women at the mall. "Remember the strawberry story?" she asked in a bit of a whisper. "It works."

I must share one more brief story about Celia, this quintessential Harlot. One evening, several of us attended a dinner dance held by a local travel group. As the music began, an elegant man who had been eyeing Celia all evening approached her. He extended his hand in an invitation to dance. "Shall we do it?" he asked. She surveyed him up and down, slowly and deliberately, looked him in the eye and responded, "Perhaps, but I think we should dance first." We all convulsed in quiet laughter while the blushing-but-grinning gentleman led her onto the dance floor.

Sensuous women throughout history have been considered intriguing and dangerous. This is in great part because, early in life, sensuality seems directly connected to the immense power of sex, and behaving sensually is a way to draw attention, attract a mate, and to bask, temporarily, in the illusion that sex and love are the same thing. Later, however, as one moves into midlife, sensuousness reveals itself as something grander and more profound.

Sensuality means living through the senses, a much more expansive kind of engagement than simply carrying out the act of sex. Women who are sensual live thoroughly aware of all that their senses tell them. It is through the senses that we take in information about the world around us; and those who are truly sensuous do not only take in such information, but also honor it by responding with energy and grace. They have learned to move in rhythm with the earth, the elements, both the subtle and the riotous beauty in nature, and the spiritual kinship among all living things.

True sensuousness is the domain of those at midlife who choose engaged sensual awareness. Because of the early focus on sexuality, many subtle sensuous experiences go unnoticed. But at the midpoint of our lives, having been invited to move our attention from the expectations of others to the comfort of our own souls, we can better notice and appreciate what our senses are telling us. Simple things— an intricate flower almost buried in tall grasses, early morning sounds that announce the day, the sensation of a graceful breeze across the skin, the way it feels to move to music—are often passed over by those younger and more concerned with climbing corporate ladders, finding sexual outlets, and establishing themselves as worthwhile members of the community. Having already done those things, we at midlife can shift awareness to the Mystery around us.

This is not to imply that women at midlife can be sensuous but not sexual; in fact, the depth of sensuousness we carry can open the door to remarkable sexual experiences. The other evening I went to a dance club where I saw a middle-aged couple do an impressive salsa routine. As I watched them move together, their eyes locked; it looked like foreplay, and I felt like a voyeur. I can only imagine what the rest of their evening involved.

The gifts of the Harlot are awareness and passion, and she expresses them in ways that are both intriguing and sometimes uncomfortable for those whose senses have lain dormant. Again, we aren't exploring sexuality here; although sensuality and sexuality can go hand in hand, they are different—and that difference is important to recognize, so let's get our terms straight. *The Oxford Dictionary* defines sexuality as "the quality of being sexual, or having sex; the capability of having sexual feelings." Pretty clear, very important, and not what we're referring to. Sensuality, on the other hand, is defined in the same dictionary as "of living beings; of or pertaining to the senses; endowed with the faculty of sensation." Equally clear, equally important, and a quality that can take its most powerful shape at the midpoint of life. In breaking down that definition, it becomes obvious that we are all sensual beings: "Of living beings" (that's you and me); "of or pertaining to the senses" (we've all got 'em); "endowed with the faculty of sensation" (we all experience sensation).

Now, you may never have thought of yourself as sensual. You may have bought into the popular concept of sensuality that involves a certain body type, seductive behavior, and the unspoken but carefully implied promise of exotic sexual experiences. That, however, as we've seen in the above definition, is not what sensuality is about. What we're talking about here is the capacity for perceiving, taking in, and interpreting information about ourselves and the world around us. It is through our senses that we experience life, and only through our senses can we learn and then implement that learning. Consider this—everything you know has come to you through your visual sense (what you see), your auditory sense (what you hear), your kinesthetic sense (what you feel, primarily physical sensations), your olfactory sense (what you smell), or your gustatory sense (what you taste). Your senses are the portals to understanding and awareness, and the degree to which you cultivate and hone them determines how much understanding and awareness you develop.

To use sensual information to its best advantage, we have to choose to be present in each moment. You may have noticed that this is a recurring theme—the Bitch, the Crone, and now the Harlot all live in a very present state, and as a result are able to readily access their power, wisdom, and sensuality. This doesn't mean the Harlot lives only for the moment and recklessly neglects lessons of the past and preparation for the future. It means that she is present to those lessons and implements them in her moment-to-moment experience, and she is equally present in the process of planning for the future. Each moment is a jewel to her, to be explored for all the information and experience it brings.

We tend to live our lives in a kind of stupor, half awake to and only partially aware of the world of experience constantly going on within and around us. This happens for several reasons: We get caught up in regret for the past and/or anticipation or dread of the future, and there is little or no energy or attention left for the present moment; we get swept away by the demands on our time and find ourselves just going through the motions of our lives, living with no hint of passion and simply focused on getting through the day, the month, the year, and eventually our entire lives. This "I'm too busy" syndrome is epidemic, and results in our neglecting the immense potential we carry, living instead at the surface level of everything, never tapping into the bottomless well of power, abundance, and joy that has been earmarked for each of us.

The third reason we spend our lives with only a dim reflection of all that is possible is that we often grow up in environments in which we learn to expect failure and disappointment, to doubt our own ideas, perceptions, and abilities, and to allow our lives to be governed by the difficulties and limitations others have taught us to anticipate. We learn not to take risks because it's too ... well, risky. We learn not to step out of the boxes our lives can become because those boxes are familiar, and familiar things feel safe even when they are slowly sucking the life out of us—remember the story of the frog who was placed in a pot of water and stayed comfortable because the environment was familiar, not realizing that as the heat was gradually turned up he was being cooked to death? And we learn not to feel, because the result of intense feelings might be pain. By the time we reach midlife, all this has been deeply impressed on our hearts, and we have a choice to make: We can continue to live lives shaped by fear and the vigilance it requires, or we can choose instead to wake up, throw off those shackles, and come out of hiding.

Now, I understand that this may sound easier said than done. After all, those things that keep us from being present in our lives are things that seem to keep us safe. Focusing on the past or future ensures that whatever is going on in my life right now won't have its full impact (since my attention is elsewhere), and that therefore, if it's difficult, scary, or sad, I won't be overwhelmed by it. If I stay too busy to explore myself on that deeper level, I don't have to worry about finding something deep within myself that I won't like. I also won't have to grapple with issues like whether I'm living with integrity, whether I have a sense of purpose in my life, and whether I am happy and at peace with who I am and how I live. And, last but certainly not least, if I avoid feeling, then maybe I can also avoid rejection, disappointment, loss, and sorrow. For those who are driven by fear there's a kind of logic present in all this. There is, however, a huge price to pay.

What if time spent regretting the past (which no longer exists) or dreading the future (which doesn't yet exist) is just wasted, time you can never regain? What if staying "too busy" keeps you powerless, and robs you of the very things you want in your life? And what if protecting yourself against disappointment, loss, and sorrow also means protecting yourself against the good stuff—the joy, love, passion, and fun you fantasize about having? What if the way to be truly safe is to take full possession of your sensual nature, to get centered and grounded in both your humanity and your divine nature, and to live as a woman whose connection to the Infinite brings with it unlimited possibilities? What if acknowledging your true spiritual heritage teaches you how to protect your heart while opening yourself to joy?

The Harlot is a woman who, at the midpoint of her life, has chosen to feel deeply, with her senses wide open, rather than to stay in that little box that promised safety but instead created a kind of physical, emotional, psychic, and spiritual distance from the happiness and excitement she really wanted. She is a woman for whom, as stated so eloquently by writer Anaïs Nin, "There came a time when the risk to remain tight in the bud was more painful than the risk it took to blossom." The Harlot may have been in touch with her own senses from birth, simply refining that awareness and taking it deeper at midlife. Or, as is more often the case, she may have spent the first half of her life in a state of sensual starvation, so overwhelmed by the demands of her life and the fear of getting lost in sensual intensity that she blocked out much of the information her senses offered.

This second situation can result in such longing to feel *something* that questionable and even dangerous options begin to look like routes of escape from the blandness that comes from neglecting the senses. The desire to feel completely is often an attempt to counter the emptiness that results from a life lived only partially present. This often takes women into perilous territory as they seek to feel satisfied, valued, even just noticed. This can be accentuated as a woman reaches middle age. As our circumstances and therefore the demands on our time and attention change, we may be forced to become very aware of just how we have muted the senses, and just how empty that has left us.

As younger women with children to care for and/or careers to develop, the demands are constant, often overwhelming, and we tend, unconsciously, to put our own sensual nature on hold because of the busyness of our lives. In the process, we lose sight of the consistent flow of information coming at us through the senses, and our experiences begin to lose their richness. We learn to go through the motions in order to get everything done that is expected of us, and going through the motions means addressing our lives in a superficial way. I often hear from younger clients that they don't have time to be present in the moment; they have too much to do, too many things to plan and prepare for; and that their attention has to be scattered among all those things, or something will fall through the cracks and there will be hell to pay. The often chaotic pace of our culture and the rigorous demands on our time, attention, and energy can make the first half of life feel like a parade of things to handle, a marathon event of gigantic proportions with no way to opt out without losing the respect of those whose expectations we are scrambling to meet.

At midlife, however, all that can change. Having managed our careers, raised our children, and jumped through countless hoops (frequently without knowing exactly why), we are seasoned and much better equipped to say "No, that doesn't work for me." The lessons learned early on make the journey out of the box much more enjoyable.

The richness of the senses is a reflection, or perhaps just a faint suggestion, of the richness of our bond with the Divine. Whether or not you are aware of that bond, it is what brings you life and what has bestowed upon you the unique essence you carry. The life force that moves through you, often thought of as *chi* or *prana,* is the evidence of that connection with Source. In choosing to quiet the mind, and perhaps using the breath to create a bridge, you can engage the senses in ways that may be different and deeper than you have experienced before. The purpose is not simply to awaken the senses, but rather to use the senses to engage more effectively, in a more rewarding way, in your life. When you relegate your senses and their constant stream of information to the back burner, you become less involved in and therefore less passionate about your world and your life. Things begin to feel less satisfying, more repetitive and unfulfilling. It is only through the senses, and in the present moment, that you can really connect with life, with your own profound essence, and with the Divine. The experiences you have through the senses provide a gateway to the much deeper realm of the spirit, which is the ultimate destination.

Another lesson the Harlot has learned as her sensuality has grown and been refined is that sensations and impressions come and go, as do the thoughts and feelings that accompany them. That means she can recognize the ebbing and flowing of sensual experiences without having to be identified by them. Her senses enrich her; they do not define her. The largely unspoken rules and expectations that structured the Harlot's earlier life have been, for the most part, dismissed at midlife. The old "shoulds" are gone. The tendency to look for approval and direction from others has been replaced by an attention toward the colors, textures, tones, scents, and tastes of her world and the many forms of satisfaction they provide. All that sensual information enhances her understanding of the direction her life might take now.

Her enhanced awareness of all that her senses reveal has generated a new mandate that she take in everything around and within her and add it all to the adventure her life continues to be.

The Harlot is committed to finding quality time for her experiences, and no longer rushes through them on the way to the next experience. She has learned to value the journey instead of just pushing to get to the destination. This is important because rushing through life and being too harried to feel means we're too busy to truly live. It means we're just going through the motions, existing instead of really living. Our self-protective busyness, and our focus on moving as quickly as possible from goal to goal without noticing the extraordinary experiences available through our senses, make life something to endure and get through rather than a journey with countless exceptional and meaningful stops along the way. When we live with our senses fully open and engaged, our perception of life changes because we feel our experiences more fully.

The Harlot has discovered, often through periods of emptiness and even broken heartedness, that her spirit is much less restless when she has found her own inner abundance. That abundance comes from her sensual awareness, the permission she's given herself to be rewarded by life, and the joy she takes in being an essential part of the divine plan. I say essential because she, like each of us, is constantly in the mind of God.

A spiritual teacher once told me that it would do me well to remember that as far as the Divine is concerned, there is no one but the two of us—God and me—and that my well-being is at the forefront of the Divine consciousness. The idea that God was focused on me as if no one else existed (and, of course, equally focused on the next person and the next and so on), and that He/She/It was concerned with my well-being absolutely floored me. I don't understand how it works, but I like it, and it has given me a whole new way to think about things. The Harlot has come to peace with this, and no longer resists the idea of being important to God. This has allowed her to create a rich inner life, filled with impressions, feelings, and ideas that take her ever deeper into the landscape of the soul. She is intrigued with life and its various dimensions, twists, and turns, and her passion for the source of that life is apparent in the way she shows up in the world.

The Harlot savors life. She looks for the gift in everything, seeks the hidden treasure in all that she encounters, and always finds it. Sometimes she savors life because she has had a wake up call that brought her to a new understanding. A friend of mine was diagnosed with cancer at age forty-eight, and as she was preparing for surgery, was told to expect the worst. In a state of shock, but choosing to trust that there was purpose and intention in this as in everything, she spent daily time in meditation and prayer, called together her family to say whatever she needed to say to them, cleaned up any loose ends, and worked to stay quiet and centered. A friend asked her why she was taking such steps if she was trusting that everything would be okay. "It's a great opportunity to clean things up," she replied. "This way, I know I'm ready for whatever happens."

I was impressed with the peace she exhibited, but I noticed that she seemed distant, as if she had begun pulling away from the reality she was facing. The surgery was performed, the prognosis was good, and her healing began. Several months later, she began reentering the social arena in which she had been so active. I saw her at several events, and the change in her was obvious. There was a glow about her, a lightness in her step, and an energy that seemed much higher than before the illness. I took her to lunch and asked about the shift I had noticed. She shared with me that after the surgery, and upon being told that the cancer was gone and her future looked strong, everything changed.

"It was as if I had been looking at my life through a lens with a big greasy thumbprint that clouded everything, and I didn't know it. I had only been partially present in everything. My energy and focus had probably always been scattered among all the things I thought required my attention. After the surgery, it was as if someone cleaned off that lens, and suddenly my life looked clear and vibrant for the first time. Colors were brighter, sounds were clearer and more melodic, sensations, smells, and tastes were all more brilliant and vital than ever before. That hasn't changed since the surgery; going through something that took me to the brink of death has awakened me to the Mystery that has always been around me, but which I hadn't been aware of before. Because of that, I can honestly say I am grateful for the cancer I experienced."

Fortunately, we don't have to be seriously ill to discover the brilliance of life. The Harlot has chosen to live in this state of awareness. Like so many other things at midlife (and actually throughout our lives), joy requires a conscious choice. We are offered that choice at every moment and in every experience. The Harlot asks the question, How do I choose to show up right now, right here? By continually questioning, she remains aware of the vast range of options from which she has to choose. It's always up to us.

When we become jaded, bored, or disillusioned and live from a place of inner scarcity, it's a quick trip to Expert Mind, the state of mind from which we think we know all there is to know. From that mindset, there is nothing new to learn, nothing fresh to experience, and nothing to take us beyond the limits of our own understanding. This way of looking at the world ensures limited opportunities, limited success, and limited happiness. Like the Crone, the Harlot lives in a state of Beginner's Mind, from which everything and everyone is experienced as if for the first time; there's always something new to discover or learn. That state of mind means she always has something to discover and look forward to. She is free from unhealthy expectations, her own and those of others, and therefore free to experience things in brand new ways. In that freedom, pleasure is always available.

When my senses are open and receptive, I can connect with all of life in a way that provides deep meaning. In that state, because I am so aware of what I am seeing, hearing, feeling, tasting, and smelling, I also become more aware of who I am and how I fit in my world. That means that living in a sensual way brings more honesty to my experiences. The more honest I am, the more present I become. The more present I become, the more passion, peace, and joy I can have. It's also true that the more present I am, the more open I become to meaningful sexual experiences because I am more aware of the possibility of connection.

It is through the senses that we can truly engage in life; and when we are so engaged, there is less room for feeling confused or stuck in old ways that no longer serve us. Remember the curiosity of the Crone? The Harlot shares that curiosity, but displays it in a different way. Her awe and wonder have to do with the sensual nature of things. She's the one who will take great pleasure in the way velvet feels on her skin, in the colors of an evening sky or a delicate blossom, the sounds, smells, and tastes all around her. She notices everything from her sensual perspective, and finds in all of it the image of the Divine. Much like the Crone and the Bitch, but in her own unique way, the Harlot finds the Sacred in everything, and each of her senses reveals to her another dimension of her God and of herself.

The Harlot's way of being isn't new to her, or to any of us. We are born sensual creatures, and over the years we allow the dampening of our sensual delight. Think about babies, and how they explore and learn about the world through the senses: They feel things, put everything in their mouths, are delighted or frightened by sounds, and intrigued by bright colors. Sensual information engages babies, and evokes from them a wide range of responses, physical and emotional. As we get older, we become distracted and sometimes ravaged by all those other things in life that seem much more important than what our senses are telling us, and, as a result, our senses get dulled. It's as if we allow a thick layer of dust to settle over them, so that even though we are still seeing, hearing, feeling, tasting, and smelling, we are no longer particularly aware of any of it, save the parts that help us survive. The Harlot's sensuality, much like a baby's, is vibrant and constant, and her cultivation of it ensures that she can thrive, not just survive.

The fingerprint of the Divine is found on all living things. It comes in different forms, different degrees of awareness, but the life force is the same. That means we are all related, bound together, life breathed into us by the source of that life. Shamans and healers throughout time have understood that connection, and have called upon the spirit inherent in all of nature to aid in the healing and transformation of a wounded planet and an ailing species. Even the heart of Gaia itself beats in rhythm with the Divine, and the Harlot feels it all. She is aware of the life that moves through everything around her, and therefore aware of her relationship to all of life. I remember a hike I took when I had really begun to pay attention to what my senses were revealing. I felt bombarded with information, but not in an overwhelming way. Everywhere I looked there was something beautiful, weird, or intriguing to see. Hidden treasures abounded, like the single flower I noticed almost hidden in a clump of tall grass, amazingly beautiful and intricate and probably missed by most people passing that way. The sounds of the forest created a perfectly timed harmony directed by something grander than itself. The feeling of the air on my skin, the rushing water of a stream on my tired feet, and the dramatic difference in temperature between the sunny areas and the shady ones had always been there, but I had never noticed them in such an intense way. In the past, I had taken this hike to have time to myself to think things out, to come up with solutions to personal or professional problems, to get away from something. This time, however, I was there to find something that was abundant in that place, the clean and fertile kind of peace present in nature.

I have always been moved by the unwavering peace and beauty found in the natural world. There is no chaos, no strife, nothing trying to be something it isn't. There are predators and prey, there is danger and death, but everything flows in the natural cadence of life. There is nothing senseless in these places, no damage done for the fun of it, no lying, cheating, deceiving, no hurting others in order to feel powerful. Everything follows its path, and it's all part of something magical.

Now, we could argue that the difference between nature and the world created by man is that humans have free will. The Harlot, however, knows that the more fundamental difference is that everything in the natural world knows its connection to the Divine, and expresses that bond in its very existence. "Knows its connection" doesn't refer to the same kind of conscious awareness we as humans have, but rather suggests an acceptance of life as it comes from the hand of God. From that place of acceptance, there is no need to struggle or resist, but rather the freedom to be fully present as part of the Divine intention. Humans, so often unaware of that sacred connection, struggle and strive, scheme and plan, and scramble to be, do, and have all sorts of things that may or may not align with Divine intention. The elements that make up the natural world, however, are simply very present in who and what they are, with no resistance, no straining to become something different. It is, perhaps, this acceptance of what is that makes these settings soothing to a frazzled human heart, and that calms inner turmoil and quiets mind chatter. A client of mine has learned to head to the mountains nearby when she feels confused or uncertain. "I always find the clarity I need when I'm hiking or skiing," she says. Insights into both personal and professional situations occur with relative ease when she can get into the quiet pace of a natural world at peace with itself. The Harlot understands this, and finds those locations where her senses, uncluttered, can provide the awareness she needs.

The connection the Harlot feels to all of life isn't limited to four-legged and two-legged life forms. She senses her connection to the earth itself, Gaia, called the Great Mother by many Native American tribes. So life springs from the hand of God, and is nurtured by the Great Mother. However, the earth can only nurture its myriad forms of life if it is being nurtured itself. This is an area where humans have fallen dramatically short.

It's difficult, even painful, to do damage to anyone or anything to which we feel truly connected. But humans have been doing great harm to the planet for generations. I am convinced that if we were deeply aware of the earth as a living entity, of our connection to her, and of the life force we have in common, we would defend her vigorously. It would not occur to us to live in ways that pollute and destroy, nor would we take natural resources for granted. This is, after all, our home. If we chose to be conscious of what the earth is constantly communicating, we could not do the damage we are doing. In the same vein, an ongoing recognition of our connection to others, however different from us they may be, might have a powerful impact on not only crime and violence, but also on our willingness to wage war. As stated by the group WildLife Associates, an organization dedicated to teaching people to care for living things and to understand the natural systems on which all life depends:

> When we learn to care about living beings other than ourselves, we begin to develop empathy and understanding of the diversity of nature and of the people around us. When we understand that natural systems sustain all life on the earth, we begin to comprehend the vital interdependence we have with all living things, including animals, plants and even the soil beneath our feet. It is then a logical step to understand that protecting nature is protecting ourselves.

The fact that there is extraordinary peace and unlimited sensual information available in natural locations doesn't mean that you have to jump into your hiking boots, strap on your backpack, and start spending lots of time in places without electricity or indoor plumbing in order to find peace and your own inherent sensuality. Urban Harlots are every bit as sensual as their nature-loving cousins. They've simply found other kinds of places they can frequent to get in touch with that deep sense of the natural rhythm of life.

The Harlot is not concerned with location, but rather with experiencing the connection she has with all living things. Over time, she has refined her awareness of the life force in its myriad forms, and has learned to take pleasure in her kinship with all. *Namaste,* a Sanskrit greeting meaning "The divine in me recognizes and honors the divine in you," is her mantra. She is grounded in the knowledge that rocks, trees, animals, growing things, people with whom, on the surface, she has nothing in common, all carry the same chi as she does, and she lives her life as a greeting to all.

It is through the senses that we connect—with each other, with ourselves, and with the Source of life. When we choose situations in which our senses tell us there is no need to compete, to protect ourselves, to be afraid, to pretend, or to prove ourselves, we are free to direct our energy toward a deeper experience of who we are in the sacred fabric of life. To this end, the Harlot knows she must periodically, even regularly, take time to replenish her sensual energy, to shake off the dust of the world and get back to the clean and open state her senses require. Getting back to that uncluttered state ensures that, however mundane her experiences may sometimes be, she will be aware of the richness hidden just beneath the surface.

I have a friend, a true Harlot, who always looks forward to doing her laundry because it's such a sensual activity for her. She takes great pleasure in noticing the different textures of the fabrics as she prepares to put a load in the washer; she loves separating the colors from the whites, because the visual contrast between the two is so rich; the fragrance of the fabric softener is heady and inviting; the whole experience gives her a bit of a sensual thrill. Is she crazy? What woman in her right mind loves to do laundry? But she isn't just doing laundry—she's giving her senses free rein, and being enriched in the process. She's an educated woman, very accomplished, very bright, and it's not as if her life is so dull that laundry is the high point. But she has chosen to take in so much more information, through the senses, so that, at this point in her life, whatever she is doing can become a rich and even intriguing experience. She looks for beauty, mystery, and wonder everywhere she goes, and she always finds it.

People who live rich, full, and rewarding lives tend to be those who get deeply involved in who they really are, the qualities they hold, the gifts they bring to life. This requires self-exploration, the willingness to uncover and address the good, the less good, and maybe even the ugly within, and a soul-level desire to be happy and at peace. So, you may be asking, who wouldn't want to be happy and at peace? Everyone wants that, don't they? Well, actually, no. As surprising as it may be, there are those who have learned to enjoy the pain and attention that being unhappy can bring. There are others who find that sorrow feels more meaningful that joy, and still others for whom unhappiness and lack have become part of their identity, and anything more positive feels unfamiliar, unnatural, and undeserved. The Harlot has transcended all of this. She is open to joy, receptive to peace, and has found her sensual temperament to be a key to a lush and vibrant inner and outer life that make both a part of her experience.

I have worked with many individuals who tell me they want to change who they are, to become someone different. "I'm a loser," I have often heard. "I'm not as good as other people, and I don't deserve to be happy." Without exception, these are people who have never fully explored themselves, who have focused only on what others have told them are their flaws, inadequacies, and failures. With only the negative and often self-serving impressions of others as a gauge for self-assessment, anyone would find herself lacking, certain that the only way to find any value in life would be to become someone more worthy. The Harlot, however, knows that each of us is wildly deserving, that our value is not based on what we have accomplished or how we measure up in someone else's eyes, but rather comes from the spiritual nature we carry into life. She is aware, also, that although our inherent value is never in question, whether we live as people of great value is entirely up to us. The quality of our lives is governed by the way we choose to express (or repress) that sacred nature, and the way we choose to perceive, interpret, and respond to our circumstances.

By deciding to immerse herself in both her internal and external experiences, the Harlot becomes more and more of who she is intended to be. Rather than finding herself inadequate, the Harlot has chosen to jump into her life like taking a leap off the high dive, and the result is invigorating.

I had a client several years ago, a bright and interesting man whose integrity was above reproach. He had a lovely family and a nice home, was deeply loved by his wife, kids, and friends, and was miserable. He was an earthy and down-to-earth kind of man, with a very practical and physical approach to life. The problem was that his wife was intent on making him a professional, a guy who wears a suit and tie, who people call "Sir" and whose line of work brings with it great respect in the professional community. "He could be anything he wants," she told me, "but he just doesn't have any ambition." What I knew was that he had tremendous ambition, just not in the direction she wanted. Hoping not to cause conflict, he ignored who he was and what he wanted, got trained in a field that left him anxious and unhappy, put on clothes that made him uncomfortable, and went to work in an office. For several months he went through the motions, trying his best to do what his wife and his boss wanted so that he could become what others regarded as successful.

He became more depressed as time went on, but was convinced that his wife knew best and that he had to hang on long enough to "make it". All this time, his own temperament, his considerable gifts and talents, and his passion were being denied, made invalid by an unfortunate choice. One day I asked a simple question I had asked before, but which he hadn't felt free to answer. "If you could do whatever you want, and money were not an issue, what would you choose?" I held my breath, waiting to see whether he would finally give himself permission to think in terms of what was right for him. He took a minute or so to consider the question, and then, slowly, his face began to light up. "I would be a carpenter," he said so quietly it was almost a whisper. "I would take a job working for someone who builds furniture, I would learn the craft very well, and then I would go out on my own. I have always wanted to work with my hands, to make something I could take pride in. That's what I would choose." The longer he spoke, the stronger his voice became, and it was obvious that what he was describing resonated deeply in him.

After a few sessions during which he learned how to find confidence and motivation, and how to trust his own judgment, he shared his desire with his wife. After her initial shock (she had never imagined herself as the wife of a craftsman), she chose, wisely, to support his ambition. Now, several years later and after lots of training, he is making a very good living, he is passionate about his work, and he enjoys his life. "He's like a different man," his wife told me when we ran into each other on the street. "He's positive, happy, and loves what he's doing. Our marriage is stronger than ever because he is so much happier."

This is not an unusual story. Any time we honor what is natural to us, and as long as we aren't doing damage in the process, we step more completely into the divine intention for our lives. We become aligned with what fits perfectly for us, and we open up to possibilities we may never have imagined. On the other hand, every moment we spend ignoring or disrespecting what is real for us is a moment during which joy, abundance, peace of mind, and various levels of success are not available to us. In that state, we are not aligned with divine intention, and we become like a damaged pipe in which the flow has been interrupted because the sections of pipe are misaligned. When my client recognized and honored what his senses, and their accompanying feelings, were telling him about what would be a fit, he moved into a state of such emotional, psychic, and spiritual congruence that what he wanted in his life could begin to flow to him.

When I speak of success, I'm not referring to the external trappings such as money, title, authority, and so on. Rather, I'm talking about the profound and comprehensive kind of success that happens internally first, and then radiates outward, positively impacting others and often resulting in those external indications of success that can make life easier and more comfortable. This internal and essence-level success, once established, becomes unwavering and shapes life in remarkable ways. This is the success that comes from self-awareness and acceptance, from choices made on the basis of that self-acceptance, from the ability and willingness to see others through the love and compassion of God, and from experiencing life in a way that constantly adds new information, with all senses wide open and receptive.

Being wide open and receptive doesn't mean a distressing and unwise degree of vulnerability. The Harlot has developed her own internal safety procedure, a system of intuitive signals that warn her away from danger and toward the relationships and experiences that are congruent with her emotional and spiritual makeup, and that guide her closer to wholeness. In her human state, the Harlot is as susceptible as everyone else to emotional ups and downs; but her well-honed inner alarm system allows her to steer away from the traps that ensnare those whose senses and accompanying intuitive insight remain underdeveloped.

Neither does "wide open and receptive" mean getting swept away by all that sensual information, and losing sight of logic and practicality. Rather than living in such a state of imbalance, the Harlot integrates everything presented by her senses with a logical and commonsensical approach, and in that way covers all the bases. Operating exclusively from logic or from her senses creates a lack of balance, and leaves her with incomplete data and limited direction. By allowing her logic and her senses to inform each other, she has everything she needs to make wise choices.

You were born with a wide range of gifts to offer to life, and the more grounded and centered you become in those gifts, choosing to be present as who you really are, the deeper and richer your experience will be. Just like my client who spent a long time feeling ashamed of his desire to do work that was both physical and creative instead of living a suit-and-tie kind of existence, many people find that a life structured according to someone else's standards is a life only partially lived. The Harlot has figured out that by simply paying attention to what comes in through the senses, she is able to get an even better grip on who she is and what works best for her. The more she understands that, the greater her self-respect and the better the choices and decisions she makes. The result is, of course, a happy, passionate, and successful life.

We are always changing, even when we aren't aware of it or making a conscious choice to do so. As life moves upon and within us, change is inevitable; there is always something new to experience, to learn, to become. Teacher and writer Deepak Chopra has said in his book *Ageless Body, Timeless Mind*:

> Quantum physics tells us that there is no end to the cosmic dance—the universal field of energy and information never stops transforming itself, becoming new at every second. Our bodies obey this same creative impulse ... In order to stay alive your body must live on the wings of change ... By the end of this year, 98 percent of the atoms in your body will have been exchanged for new ones.

This idea of constant and inevitable change applies equally to our bodies, minds, and spirits, and the Harlot knows that resistance is futile. She can try to stand her ground and refuse to change, but the pace of change is inescapable. Thumbing her nose at it will only result in her being dragged along, kicking and screaming, and getting bruised up in the process. Therefore, no matter how comfortable she is at any moment in time, she is ready for whatever comes next. Many of the changes that shape our lives and contribute to the power of midlife concern the shifts in perspective and response that occur from one time of life to another as priorities, criteria, and focus transform.

Early in life, before developing a solid basis for living with grace and sensual savvy, it's common to interpret any and maybe all emotions and sensations as signals to eat something, drink something, take a drug, or have sex. Or perhaps, during the first half of life, emotions and sensations often serve as excuses to indulge in behaviors designed to change an uncomfortable state, or enhance a better one. This was certainly the case for me early in life. If I felt sad or lonely, I could eat, drink, self-medicate, or get temporarily lost in a sexual encounter, and maybe (or maybe not) come out feeling less sad or lonely. If I felt happy, even exhilarated, I could eat, drink, self-medicate, or temporarily lose myself in a sexual encounter as a way to celebrate and maybe come away feeling even better. Either way, my interpretation remained the same: Feeling something, good or not, physical or emotional, meant it was time to indulge in something. Of course, the same thing applied to not feeling, or feeling empty. Indulgence of the types mentioned was often the method I used to try to feel *something* rather than nothing. As you might imagine, this philosophy pretty much covered everything. Feel good, feel bad, feel nothing at all ... indulgence was the answer. The difficulty is that, for most of us, those forms of indulgence often brought a price to pay—addiction, hangovers, unwanted pregnancy, STDs, embarrassment—and rarely served in the ways we hoped they would.

The Harlot, having lived half or more of her life, having experimented with all that unproductive indulgence, and having constructed a very different way of interpreting and approaching her life, now understands her emotional and sensual experiences in another way altogether. Her commitment now is to recognize her emotions and sensations as messengers pointing out that there is something to which she must pay attention. Physical sensations draw her awareness to what the body needs; emotional response offers information regarding her current state, what she needs to strengthen in herself, and how actively aware of the Divine within she may be. As she allows herself to feel what she's feeling and acknowledge those feelings, her world and the world around her expand. With every sensual experience and her grasp of its meaning, it's as if she grows more fully into her own skin, taking deeper possession of everything that is intended for her.

There are several factors that move the Harlot at the midpoint of her life to begin embracing her feelings instead of ignoring or denying them. In doing so, her life becomes a more honest and powerful expression of who she is, and that allows her to get to that present state that may have eluded her to that point. From that place of presence, she can be open to a range of experiences that is richer and a lot more rewarding than what she is used to. She is careful to release her emotions after acknowledging them, in order not to get stuck, because she knows that if she hangs on to them, either by continuing to re-experience them or by denying them altogether, she puts herself at the mercy of those feelings, and they begin to negatively impact the quality of her life.

Another reason the Harlot chooses to take ownership of her inner experience is that after years of working so hard to fit in, to be accepted and found worthy, and to live in a way that leaves out the power and intensity of her sensual inner wiring, she may have just gotten tired of it. At midlife, it's likely that she's reached her saturation point. Whereas a woman less in tune with herself might feel like throwing in the towel and giving up, the Harlot reaches that saturation point and says, "Okay, it's time to get real. It's time to show up, to live large, alive, awake, and ready to rock." Instead of surrendering to the world of hair nets, sensible shoes, and a bleak future at midlife, the Harlot uses this time of life to unlock the vibrancy that's been there all along. She may or may not buy new clothes, get a facial, explore the wonderful world of makeovers, or learn to tango. But however she goes about the unlocking, it begins within. Often, in response to the onset of middle age, women will rush out to change the exterior without realizing that it's an attitude thing, an inner issue instead. You can get the new clothes, new hairstyle, lose weight, even find a new lover or husband, but it won't be enough to make this time of life the sexy and joyful rite of passage it's intended to be. The true transformation happens within, and once that's occurred the wardrobe, makeup, and anything else you choose to explore are icing on the cake.

The third reason the Harlot chooses to pay attention to her inner experience is that she has learned what happens when she doesn't, and she doesn't want to waste her time and energy in that way any longer. She's figured out that holding back and denying what's real for her is an act of self-betrayal, a kind of disowning of the self. She realizes that living this way weakens her sense of her value, and she's no longer willing to do that.

If you have children, you may remember what it's like when they reach the age of two. They clamor for your attention, especially when they realize that you're focused on something else and not noticing them. They need reassurance that you are still present for them, that they are still important to you, that they are safe. The longer your ignore them, tell them to be quiet, push them away, the louder their demands become. Often all it takes to calm their concerns is a few seconds of attention. By simply being acknowledged, they are once again happy and reassured, and you can return to what you were doing. It works much the same way with aspects of ourselves. The longer we ignore or deny them, the more uncomfortable and unhappy we may become, the more empty we may begin to feel. The neglected parts begin demanding the attention they need more and more loudly, and life begins to feel chaotic. The Harlot understands how this applies to her inner experiences, and knows that she must give her senses their due. By recognizing that she is such a sensual being, and that having her senses open and receptive is essential to her joy, by giving that aspect of herself expression—especially at midlife, when earlier she may not have—the Harlot's world broadens and she feels as if she's come home.

The Harlot is a woman for whom pleasure is of great importance, however she is not at all a hedonist. For hedonists, the pursuit of pleasure for its own sake is paramount and other things, including people, take a backseat. For the Harlot, pleasure is not the goal but is rather a byproduct of the state of presence in which she chooses to live. Pleasure is a gauge by which she can measure her awareness of the divine presence all around her. That the Divine is present is not in question; her awareness of that presence may come and go, depending on where she has chosen to place her focus. Pleasure is a given, part of the grand scheme, and is always available. The challenge is for us to pay close enough attention to find it.

Just a bit of clarification here: When I refer to pleasure, I'm not talking about sex—although I'm firmly in favor of sexual pleasure. On a planet where sex is used with increasing frequency to sell, to persuade, and to entice, it's easy to figure that pleasure belongs to the sexual realm. In reality, however, sexual pleasure is a subset of the much grander pleasure I mentioned above, the pleasure that is available in a state of full presence. When we are distracted, our attention and energy scattered in many directions, we simply don't notice many (maybe most) of the things that could offer pleasure to the senses. We deprive ourselves of the enjoyment that is possible, and that I believe is intended for us, simply by not paying attention. When, on the other hand, we bring full awareness to whatever we're doing, we suddenly realize that the senses are constantly being bombarded with wonderful stuff that can convey a level of pleasure we may have lost sight of, or perhaps never known.

I recently had an experience that was a great example of this. It was early spring, and finally warm enough to take long walks comfortably. I was walking in my neighborhood one morning, distracted by several things weighing on my mind, and I began to notice that just about everyone I saw walking in the area was talking on a cell phone. For a brief moment I marveled at how willing people were to scatter their attention and in the process miss so much of what was going on around them. And then it dawned on me—I had been doing the same thing; walking past trees heavy with fragrant cherry or apple blossoms, too caught up in what was going on in my head to notice the beauty around me. Birds were singing in that clear, early morning way, but I had missed it because my attention was elsewhere. I was going to miss out on the way new leaves on bushes feel to the touch because the things rolling around in my head were in the way. Realizing how unaware I had been, and how much pleasure I was missing, I spent the remainder of my walk amazed by just how extraordinarily gorgeous life becomes in the spring. I touched petals and leaves. I listened to how different each bird's song was. I appreciated colors and smelled blossoms. By the time I got home, I was in a state of wonder, even delight, and the issues I had dragged with me at the beginning of my walk had begun to look different. In truth, the issues were the same; it was me, my perspective that had changed. And that, in turn, changed everything.

Pleasure is not the only reason for the Harlot's conscious choice, each day and every moment, to live with her senses open, ready to receive the information available all around her. She understands that in that state of sensual acuity she sees more, listens and hears at a deeper level, notices things other people miss, and picks up on quiet, often unspoken, clues and other subtleties she wouldn't discern if she were caught up in the head stuff that can distract and demand attention. The ability to notice these often-missed aspects of any situation means that she has a great deal more information to go on as she makes choices and decisions, as she finds within her the most resourceful response, and as she takes action. This allows her to stay on track more consistently, and to move forward in ways that truly take her where she wants to go, instead of living a trial-and-error kind of life. The result is greater reward, increased abundance, and more joy.

We talked earlier about how, in nature, there is great acceptance for what is. Rocks don't wish they were trees, mountain lions don't resent their state and wish they had been born grizzlies, everything is deeply involved in what is and what is intended to be. That acceptance is essential if we want to find peace, however it works a bit differently for humans. It's important to understand that accepting what is does not mean choosing not to move toward an ever-increasing level of excellence. There is nothing noble or superb about living a life that is less than excellent, and choosing to do nothing to change it. The "I hate my job, I'm always broke, and I'm in an abusive relationship, but it's important to accept what is, so I guess I'll stay here" approach to life doesn't work for any of our archetypes. Accepting what is doesn't include tolerating negative or harmful situations; it means, for our purposes, accepting that you're a middle-aged woman, and choosing to become the best darn middle-aged woman you can possibly be.

I've know many women who expend lots of energy resenting their female-ness, and wishing they had been born male so life would be easier. What a complete waste of time and focus. They can't change their gender, and would likely find the result to be a great disappointment if they could. These women, and all of us, can instead decide to manifest their gifts so fully that they become extraordinary individuals. Gender isn't the point. It's the choice to move into the "extraordinary" part that will change our lives, and ultimately transform our planet. The Harlot lives with an eye to ever increasing excellence in her life. The goal that underlies everything she does is to become the best she can be, and she knows that whatever she's doing can be done with such quality and commitment that it becomes a startling expression of everything she is capable of being. She doesn't see life as a competitive event, so her desire to improve has nothing to do with being better than others. She knows there is no end to what she can experience and accomplish, that there are unlimited layers to explore within, and that when she is in full possession of who she was created to be, she becomes a true expression of the Divine on earth.

So what about sex? What part does sex play for the Harlot who, as a middle-aged woman, lives such a sensual life? At the midpoint of life, sex takes on a different meaning and purpose than it had when we were younger. Most of us probably spent years with sex as a way to vie for attention, to draw others into relationship, to feel loved and desired, to express a depth of emotion we shared with someone significant in our lives, and as the way to reproduce and move into the role of parent and responsible adult. Now, after everything we've learned through the first half of our lives, sex can become a vehicle for a different kind of connection and meaning.

Sex at midlife is still a remarkable way to express love and affection, and to create and deepen the closeness we may have in our relationships. At this point, however, having developed a clearer and expanded sense of self as we moved from challenge to challenge in our earlier lives, sex no longer serves as a way to get attention and to feel desirable. This is true for several reasons, not the least of which is that we have begun to let go of the need for attention in order to feel okay. We have seen ourselves handle numerous things, deal with a wide range of situations and come through them wiser and stronger, and we have half a lifetime of evidence indicating that we are far beyond just okay.

Another reason we are less likely at midlife to use sex as an enticement is that we've had time to learn a lot about relationships and how they work. That doesn't mean we've necessarily gotten really good at it yet, but we've had enough experience to begin to put the pieces together and put sex in its place. Whether we've had a series of temporary relationships, or a marriage that's lasted for years, as we have evolved, sex has probably moved from the central position to one of greater balance.

As younger women, we may have bought into the idea that the passion and sexual excitement we felt early in a relationship would last, would never change its shape, and would be the glue to hold the relationship together, especially during tough times. At midlife, we know better. We've seen passion come and go, we may have been in situations in which sex that once was mind-blowing has become mundane, and we've learned that it's only through developing connection at a deeper level that any relationship has the opportunity to become something of true substance. Having learned this, the Harlot recognizes sex as a byproduct of connection, not the purpose. She also knows that, generally speaking, the deeper the connection, the greater the potential for terrific sex. Therefore, for her, the connection comes first. She has developed great skill in seeing, hearing, and feeling the possibility of such connection, and doesn't waste her time and energy in places where that possibility doesn't exist. Anyone who wants to have sex first, and get to know who she is later, doesn't have a chance.

At this midpoint in life, hormonal changes contribute to a shift in the status of sex in a relationship. Sexual response may be slower, orgasms may be less intense, and changes in your body may have brought with them a degree of self-consciousness that makes comfortable and uninhibited sex less likely. But there are ways to address this: Hormone replacement therapy (HRT) can help bring your estrogen closer to its earlier level, and increase sex drive, and there are natural approaches if you don't want the possible side effects that are concerns with HRT. Weight gain, body parts that have begun to sag, and stretch marks can all make it difficult to feel as sexy as you want to feel, and this is where the sensuality of the Harlot is so important.

Harlots come in all shapes and sizes, but their sensual awareness isn't diminished by the physical changes that can take place as they hit middle age. It's the Harlot's attitude that makes her sexy, not the distribution of body fat. As sensitive as she is to sensual information, she can focus on giving pleasure—and she receives pleasure as a result.

As stated elegantly by Jim Morrison of the American band The Doors, "Blake said that the body was the soul's prison unless the five senses are fully developed and open. He considered the senses the 'windows of the soul'. When sex involves all the senses intensely, it can be like a mystical experience."

Spending time in what could be delicate conversations with your partner to determine what works best, what feels best, what each of you needs in order to make your sexual experiences as satisfying as possible can lead to a shift in the way you approach sex and each other. Making intimate touch, rather than orgasm, the goal can take the pressure off and allow things to take what may be a new and exciting direction.

I've spoken with many people for whom sex has become a non-issue at midlife. It may have lost its appeal over the course of a long relationship—which is not inevitable, but happens when people stop paying attention—or perhaps there is no relationship within which sex can occur. Perhaps resentment has become a barrier that precludes a sexual expression of love. Or maybe both partners have allowed the day-to-day stuff of life, and the fatigue that can be part of it, to overwhelm their natural desire. Whatever the cause, neglecting the sexual aspect of a meaningful relationship is never wise. That neglect leaves a gap, both emotional and physical, that nothing else can fill. Research indicates that sex encourages the release of substances that strengthen the immune system, releases natural painkillers, reduces anxiety, strengthens the heart and lungs, improves circulation, and promotes relaxation and a sense of well-being. Having good sex, especially with someone to whom you feel close, can result in feeling desired and sexy, and that enhances self-esteem. Sex is an integral part of any healthy relationship, whatever the ages of the partners. Taking conscious action to maintain and strengthen that connection can dramatically enhance both physical and emotional health, while providing an inexpensive way to have a very good time.

If you find your sexual energy and interest flagging, rather than figuring that it's just time to slow down the flow of those juices, you can choose to take action that can help re-energize and re-stimulate this vital part of who you are. Speak with your doctor and get your hormone levels checked. Have an intimate conversation with your partner to express your feelings and brainstorm together ways to fire it up again. Sometimes it's helpful to work with a professional who specializes in sexual matters, someone whose view of your sex life is uncluttered by any old wounds or self-consciousness that may be getting in your way. Couples can often get some great new ideas by letting an objective stranger explore their situation with them. And, no, I'm not suggesting an expensive romp in the hay with a sexual surrogate; there are many counselors who are trained to work with couples who want to rekindle their sexual connection, and to help them see and respond to that part of their relationship with renewed passion. The important thing is not to resign yourself to a future that neglects an entire aspect of who you are. While sex may not be as all consuming at midlife as it once was, it will always be an exceptional way to express yourself, and to connect deeply with someone you love. It is, perhaps, at the midpoint of life and beyond that patience, tenderness, and the desire to give pleasure are most important.

Many women grew up laboring under a variety of myths regarding sexuality, beauty, fertility, and femininity. These myths, when accepted, can make the first half of life feel like a constant competition, and the second half feel like a discouraging downward spiral. So, let's bust some myths, shall we?

As young girls, we often learn to confuse beauty with the right to be loved. It's usually an unspoken lesson, but we learn early to figure that it's the beautiful ones who deserve to be loved, the pretty ones who can stimulate the feeling of love in others, and that if we don't fit the generally-accepted standard of beauty, we aren't as worthy of love. This is a devastating concept when we are younger, one that brings loneliness and the feeling that our only value lies in our appearance. At midlife, if we have spent years resenting or envying those we regarded as more attractive and therefore more deserving, it becomes more difficult to discover the profound and soul-level beauty we carry within.

This is a myth that can hurt and limit us, and create pain and confusion for those individuals who put themselves at the mercy of beautiful women, and then find that physical beauty doesn't necessarily bring with it other attributes of value. It puts me in mind of a line from a song that was popular several years ago, and that was much wiser than its writer and performer, Robert Palmer, may have realized: "A pretty face don't make no pretty heart" says it all. Beauty, kindness, spiritual awareness, and passion aren't mutually exclusive, but they don't automatically come together in the same package either. It would serve us well to explore the whole person—ourselves as well as those around us—and to choose our companions on the basis of the entire picture instead of the one or two attributes we initially find most attractive.

You deserve to be loved because you exist. Money, beauty, popularity, perky breasts, and all the other often quirky criteria established by society as important do not earn love—not real love anyway. Love is your birthright; because you have sprung from the hand of the Divine and carry that nature within, and because the Divine is the author of love, it seems obvious that you were shaped by love, and you have always deserved love. Your task is not to struggle to earn love, but rather to remember your true nature and begin living it.

Another myth that has an impact on our quality of life as we hit middle age is that we are most feminine while we are fertile, and menopause, marking the end of our childbearing years, also marks the end, or at least an unattractive dwindling, of our femininity. This implies that femininity is the product of certain hormones, which is untrue. Libido is certainly linked to but not entirely determined by hormone levels, but libido and femininity are different things.

Femininity, in its truest form, has to do with how we think. Men and women are wired differently, and there are actually structural differences between the male and female brains.[2] We think differently, we focus on different things, we respond differently to life's experiences. "Female" is as much as way of viewing things and showing up in the world as it is a matter of anatomy. Our femininity (whatever that means to you) can only be diminished by our own disrespecting of who we are. If we decide that once we can no longer fulfill the role of child bearer then we are less feminine than those who can, that will become our truth and our lives will reflect that belief in the experiences we draw into our sphere. On the other hand, when we realize that everything that has brought us into our power, wisdom, and sensuality has enhanced our femininity, our lives will be filled with events and relationships that express the mystical feminine that we embody.

We are always fertile, but in different ways at different stages of our lives. The word "fertile" has several definitions, only one of which refers to bearing offspring. Its other definitions include "abundantly productive" and "fruitful". This is a clear indication that fertility is not limited to those who still ovulate. The end of our ability to reproduce does not signal the loss of fertility, but instead announces a change in its form. We are fertile because we are alive, and life is fertile; we are fertile ground at every phase of our lives. At midlife it may be time to quit having babies, and to begin having new ideas, new experiences, and great adventures, to learn new things, develop new skills, get creative ... Those are all products of our lifelong and inherent fertility.

The femininity to which I am referring has nothing to do with makeup, ruffles and bows, or the color pink; it has to do with being willing to be fully, powerfully female. It comes from being totally immersed in that female-ness, instead of skimming across the surface of our lives and never really getting to the magic that happens when a woman has the courage to give the mystical feminine free reign.

The other myth I'd like to blow holes in is one that was alluded to earlier, but that bears repeating. This is the myth that sexual activity and libidinous thoughts are intended primarily, even exclusively, for the first half of life, when both lust and fertility run high. The truth, as I've already stated, is that the purpose of sex at midlife is no longer procreation, but instead to connect, to feel close, and to express who we are becoming as we evolve in power, wisdom, and sensuality. We have something different to express now, something that goes beyond feeling horny or hoping to start a family. There is nothing wrong or superficial about either horniness or the desire to have babies; I've enjoyed both. However, it's different now. I am different now, and what I choose to communicate sexually has changed. I am no longer trying to prove anything, not vying for attention, not hoping to perform well enough to elicit a commitment. Now I am just me, offering a wonderful experience to someone I care for, and getting the same in return. What tremendous freedom there is in that.

So for those of us at midlife, sex can be a great form of recreation, a pleasant addition to our exercise program, inexpensive entertainment, a terrific stress reducer, and most importantly, an unparalleled tactile love song. It's such a gift—why would we ever want to give it up?

People often confuse the Harlot with common, everyday sex symbols; but the two are very different. Was Marilyn Monroe a Harlot? Mae West? These were women who titillated and enticed, whose implied promise of sexual delights without emotional attachment was the substance of many men's fantasies. I can't speak for their sensual awareness, but I am certain that our Harlot doesn't need to thrust her sexuality on others, or to find her sense of self through her sexuality. I am not judging individuals whose identity is strongly sexual, simply pointing out the important difference between them and the Harlot.

Individuals who present themselves in an overtly sexual manner might be considered vampish or flirtatious, and at least some of the behaviors that are so obviously sexual may be prompted by information coming at them through their senses. They are different, however, from the Harlot in that there is typically a self-serving agenda lurking behind the alluring presentation: a strong drive for attention, a yearning to feel important and desired, the need to be validated by others. We can perhaps all understand what it's like to feel those things, but the Harlot has moved beyond them. Rather than using her sensuality to get attention, this woman is in it for the joy and the connection to the Mystery that reveals itself a bit at a time through her senses. This is one of the reasons that self-awareness and acceptance are so important; because the Harlot has come to appreciate and validate herself, she no longer has to spend time and energy trying to get appreciation and validation from others. She is free to focus that time and energy on the sensual input that informs her world.

Sometimes, when we have become accustomed to feeling bad, or not feeling at all, the prospect of living through the senses can be intimidating. What if I let myself notice all that sensual stuff and get so caught up in it that I lose control? What if I'm kidding myself by thinking that sensual acuity could open new doors and help me feel better? What if there's just never enough time to get real about myself and my life? Isn't it safer to shut out everything I can't control and live on automatic pilot? What if I'm too old/bored/lonely/fat/thin/average to be sensual?

These are all fear-based questions, and if any of these questions occur to you, it may be time to give up the fear and replace it with possibility. This is a great time for that powerful question (What if ...?) as it applies to your future. What if the second half of my life could be even more remarkable than the first? What if I can live filled with and surrounded by beauty and opportunity? What if I *am* worthy?

Joy can't be corralled, loved can't be controlled, passion can't be regulated. Several years ago, during a very painful time in my life, a dear friend told me that it was time to abandon myself to joy. The concept took my breath away. To abandon myself to joy would require giving up all the elaborate steps I had taken to protect myself, to ensure that I was safe. And then I realized that all my efforts to protect myself against pain had also effectively protected me against the joy she was suggesting. Pain or joy? The choice was, and had always been, mine.

4

Getting There

You carry within you the seeds of your own Bitch, Crone, and Harlot. They've always been there, but until now they were probably a bit unformed, undefined, and not yet evolved enough for full and meaningful expression. There has been so much to learn, so many pieces of the puzzle to put together so the image of You as Exceptional and Cherished Woman could emerge. Whether you have been aware of it or not, you were learning all the time, in every situation, and adding the lessons, the conclusions you reached, to your perspective on life. Midlife is the perfect time for your own personal "reveal": the discovery, unwrapping, and presentation of the evolved you in all your power, wisdom, and sensuality.

As we have seen throughout our exploration of midlife archetypes, it is not automatic that women entering middle age become powerful, wise, and/or sensual. The decision to peel back the layers that have been accumulating and masking those life-shaping attributes requires courage and the willingness to do life differently. But once your own precious Bitch, Crone, and Harlot recognize that they are, perhaps for the first time, welcome in your experience, living your power, wisdom, and sensuality will feel like the most natural act you've ever performed.

You may not be feeling particularly powerful, wise, or sensual, especially if you've spent the first half of your life taking care of everyone but yourself. In fact, it may seem as if youth is disappearing fast—and with it any opportunity to feel vital, sexy, and to have a real impact in the world. You may be thinking that the Bitch, the Crone, and the Harlot are aspects of other women, but not you. Let me assure you, they're all in there waiting for you to invite them to show up.

Issuing that invitation to these extraordinary parts of yourself requires a very specific way of thinking, and it may feel challenging at first. Remember the concept that we create our own reality; whatever we repeatedly focus our thoughts on we give life to, and we draw to ourselves experiences that reflect that focus. If you are used to thinking of yourself as less important than other people, or as someone who gets taken advantage of by others, you have probably been having lots of experiences that seem to confirm that concept. If that's been the case, then you may feel strange, even guilty at first about focusing on what you want or need, and on how you can best make sure your energy is always replenished. However, the truth is that this way of thinking isn't selfish; rather, it is the smart and productive way to understand who you are. You spend a lot of time and energy giving, and taking responsibility for all sorts of things, and we've talked about how quickly we move into a state of physical, emotional, and spiritual depletion when we don't take action to get refueled. That doesn't serve us or anyone else, and it can lead to either exhaustion and illness, or resentment and whininess. Neither of those states can usher us into a powerful, wise, and sensual midlife.

You already have everything you need to manifest your Bitch, Crone, and Harlot, but if you don't know how to access and give expression to each of these, it won't happen. Once you have the tools to bring them to the surface, however, to offer them as gifts to the world, the possibilities are truly endless.

One of the initial steps toward our archetypes is to ask that magical question: What if ...? This is a question we'll ask frequently on the path toward a rich and remarkable future. We've already looked at how this simple question begins loosening our death grip on beliefs that have kept us stuck in old and limiting ways of living. But letting go of old beliefs isn't enough; we need to replace them with beliefs that support who we really are, and what we really want. If we just release the old without putting the new in its place, we create an empty space within that has to get filled—and it usually gets filled with the old stuff again because that's what feels familiar. The New Testament offers a great example: In both the gospels of Matthew and Luke, Christ tells the story of a man who had been cleansed of an unclean spirit. This unclean spirit, having gotten used to dwelling in this man's heart, wandered around looking for a new place to live. Finding none, it decided to return to its former dwelling place (the man it had inhabited earlier). Upon returning to its old host, the spirit found that the man had been through a nice process of emotional spring cleaning, and was one big empty space, never having replaced the old inhabitant with anything better. That clean, open space was very inviting; the spirit gathered seven of its pals, and they all took up residence in the unfortunate guy.[1] By not replacing the old with something that served him better, this man ended up worse off than he had been before. Now, there may be those who would accuse me of taking license with this very important story; I, however, find it to be an excellent example of exactly what we're talking about. If we're going to let go of something that hurts and limits us, we'd better be ready to replace it with something that will move us successfully toward our intended outcome. If we don't, we'll likely slide right back into our old ways, and maybe even worse.

As you already know, everything we create in our lives begins with our beliefs, and our circumstances are always reflecting back to us whatever it is we have learned to believe is true. To shape middle age so that it radiates sacred alignment and divine intention, it's essential to begin by taking an honest look at the beliefs that have, to this point, molded our lives. But just getting clear about what those beliefs are and how they may have held us back isn't enough. Once we have recognized them, we can release and replace, and begin creating something different.

So, how can you change beliefs that may have held you back and kept you from the life you want to live? Is it even possible to let go of such limitations and replace them with new beliefs that can move you toward the mindset of these archetypal figures? What if your life has been so thoroughly shaped by negative beliefs that nothing more positive feels available? The kind of life-limiting beliefs I'm referring to include things like:

- I'm not good enough.
- I don't deserve love/happiness/abundance/success/peace.
- I could never be successful.
- No one worth loving would ever want me.
- Life is really hard.
- There isn't enough.
- Something terrible is going to happen.
- Anything good I might get will be taken away from me.
- There's something wrong with me.
- God doesn't love me.

As you can see, given that our beliefs shape what we experience, these beliefs and others like them can only draw to us some pretty unhappy times. Our three archetypes allow no space for such ideas, and are careful to monitor the assumptions and notions to which they give attention and therefore life. They understand the connection between what goes on in their heads and what goes on in their lives, and they make intentional choices that focus on what they want and who they are. By way of further clarification, it's important to know a bit about the Law of Attraction, which is the principle governing that connection. As we discussed earlier, the generally accepted definition of this law is that things of like vibration are drawn to each other. Another way of expressing it is that:

- When you expect something, it's on its way to you.

- When you believe something, that belief draws it to you.

- When you fear something, it immediately heads toward you.

That means that entertaining negative thoughts results in attracting negative experiences and people into your world. Giving attention to things and events you're afraid of will draw to you those very things, and effective concentration on what you do want will magnetize it to you.

As I have already mentioned, by focusing your thoughts you become like a very powerful magnet. But there's an interesting twist to consider: By focusing on the absence of what you want, you perpetuate that absence. Let me explain. Let's say you want and need more money—there are bills you can't pay, lots of anxiety, your self-esteem is suffering. By spending time and energy thinking about how little money you have and how you need to have more, you are actually focusing on the absence of what you want, and that will perpetuate that absence. This means that you'll continue not having enough because you are focused on the fact that you don't! According to this law, there is no such thing as exclusion. You can't exclude what you don't want by thinking about how much you don't want it. Whatever you're concentrating on, positive or negative, will be drawn to you.

I'm not talking about occasional thoughts that come and go, but rather the things you keep coming back to in your head. The thoughts, assumptions, and beliefs you entertain regularly quickly begin to feel very natural, and it's easy to slide back into them with little or no provocation. It's at that point that such thoughts become powerful enough to draw people and experiences of the same vibration into your life.

Thoughts repeated often soon become assumptions, and assumptions quickly become beliefs. Beliefs form the foundation of everything we create in our lives. I bring this up because our three archetypes have learned to monitor their beliefs, and to disallow any that might prevent them from being all they are intended to be. A woman who has learned to believe she isn't powerful enough to make worthwhile things happen can't discover and welcome her Bitch. The woman who has bought into the idea that she has no wisdom and that she can't trust her own judgment can't uncover and express her Crone. And a woman who has been convinced by others that she's too old, too fat, too thin, too plain, too unimportant ever to be considered sensual (or that sensuality at midlife is inappropriate) will find that her Harlot remains in a deep sleep.

This being the case, it's essential to examine your existing beliefs, root out any that have kept you in a holding pattern in life, and replace them with beliefs that bring the power to step firmly into your birthright. The following is a process designed by Robert McDonald, an NLP practitioner in California, to help change limiting beliefs. It allows you to actually experience what it's like to let go of such a limitation and replace it with a new belief that can move you toward the mindset of these archetypal figures. You can do this by yourself, or ask a trusted friend to walk you through it. This will help you release any beliefs that don't get you where you want to be, and exchange them for new ones that align with who you really are. The process goes like this:

1. Identify a belief you currently hold that may be limiting you, keeping you from creating what you want.

2. Come up with a belief you would rather have, your Preferred Belief. A good way to find this Preferred Belief is to ask yourself, "What would I have to believe in order to create what I want?" When you have identified this new belief, state it in a positive way and with passion. Make sure this new

belief is yours, not one someone else thinks you should have. Make sure also that it's a belief you can implement in your life, and that it's respectful of others. This new and preferred belief must be about progress, not perfection.

3. Make six labels for each of six locations on the floor. These locations will represent stages of change for you. The six labels should say Current Belief, Open to Doubt, Museum of Old Beliefs, Preferred Belief, Open to Believing, and The Sacred Place.

4. Place these labels on the floor in a clockwise order.

5. In your mind, set up a kind of anchor for each location. That means that as you move around the labels, stepping from one to the next, you think of an experience from your life that fits each label description.

6. Stand in the Current Belief position and experience your limiting belief. Notice how this belief leaves you feeling.

7. Taking your limiting belief with you, step from the Current Belief location to the Open to Doubt position. As you do, notice how you feel now that you are open to doubting that limiting belief. This is a great place to ask that powerful question: What if ...? What if that old belief isn't true? What if I just thought it was true, but it was never really the case?

8. Step into the Museum of Old Beliefs, taking with you that old and doubted belief.

9. Leave the old belief at the Museum of Old Beliefs, and move into your Preferred Belief location. Now notice how you feel stepping into your Preferred Belief without the old limiting belief to hold you back.

10. Now, move with your Preferred Belief into the Open to Believing location. Feel yourself being open to believing that this Preferred Belief is true. This is another great place for

What if ...? What if this new belief really is true? What if I do deserve love? What if what I want really is available to me?

11. Take your Preferred Belief into the Sacred Space Location. This position allows you to integrate your new belief so that it becomes part of you.

12. Complete the process by feeling your now accepted and integrated Preferred Belief as you step into the Current Belief location. Notice what you experience as you stand once again in the Current Belief position, but this time with your Preferred Belief as the Current Belief. That Preferred and Current Belief can now form the foundation for what you create in your everyday experiences. And when your beliefs open the door to what you want, the sky's the limit.

Take a moment now to consider how you feel with the old and limiting belief gone, and the Preferred Belief in its place. How does this new belief affect your perception of yourself? How much more possible does it seem to become your own Bitch, Crone, and Harlot now that you hold a belief that supports what you want? How will this new and preferred belief influence the way you live and the actions you take?

Take a few minutes and explore this process. It's simple, doesn't take long, and its impact can be profound. This can be done any time you find yourself being limited by a belief that doesn't move you forward. You may be quite surprised at the ways life can change when your underlying beliefs shift.

Remember that your ability to create the kind of life you want, and to contribute to the quality of life on the planet, is shaped by the way you think. Think like a powerful woman, and you become a powerful woman; regard life as a wise woman does, and you become wise; experience life through all your senses, and you become sensual. So once you've worked with your beliefs, it's important to have the tools you need to develop a way of thinking that matches those positive archetypes of midlife. It will be worthwhile to look at a few simple ways you can step into the world and way of thinking of the Bitch, the Crone, and the Harlot.

Finding Your Bitch

You may remember that the gifts of the Bitch are Power and Possibility, and that the way she responds to her world is a constant reflection of that potent combination.

The Bitch has had all the same challenges in life as all the rest of us, and at any point in time she could have retreated from difficult situations, curled up in fetal position, and whined, "I can't, it's too hard." But she didn't—and as a result of her willingness to keep going and her commitment to make a difference, her life is a showcase of what is possible when women choose to live their power.

Courage, confidence, and clarity are a few of the qualities that make the Bitch who she is, and fortunately those qualities are available to every woman who wants them. However, developing these characteristics doesn't happen over night—they have to be trained and cultivated, much like muscles that only grow stronger when you use them well. The cultivation of these qualities often happens best in gradual increments. Just like building muscles at the gym, small steps work best and go a long way toward preventing mistakes, injury, and disappointment. For the Bitch, courage, confidence, and clarity go hand in hand, each informing the other. Without clarity, she can't see the optimal outcome or the path that will get her there; without courage, she may see what needs to be done, but she won't feel brave enough to do it; and without confidence, she can't possibly be open to either courage or clarity. So, she needs all three, and confidence is a great place to start.

You know what it's like to be confident. Now, you may be disputing this wildly, thinking, "What's she talking about? I've never been confident. If I knew how to be confident, my whole life would be different." But I stand by my statement. You have had times in your life when you felt certain that you knew what to do and how to do it. It might have been some really significant and perhaps unusual experience, or maybe it was simply knowing that you're a great cook, a terrific parent, or someone who has created a warm and welcoming home. Whatever it has been, you have had at least a taste of the confidence that is fundamental to the power of the Bitch. Now it's time to recapture that feeling, apply it to your everyday life, and let it begin to shape your experiences.

The lack of confidence usually comes from troublesome, often distorted memories of past events. While you can't change what happened, you can change its meaning to you in the present and its effect on how you feel and the behaviors you choose. Once you've changed the meaning of past events, your confidence can begin to take its rightful place. This simple technique will help you get started:

1. Think of a situation from the past that would have gone very differently if you had been really confident. Go back to that past event as if you were there again, seeing what you saw, hearing what you heard, and doing what you did at that time. Notice what feelings you have as you re-experience that situation.

2. Count backwards and out loud from 100 to 73 by threes (100, 97, 94, and so on).

3. Now, think of a specific situation when you were confident and certain of your ability to deal with whatever was going on.

4. Step back into that situation as if it were happening again. Feel the confidence building, and when it's at its peak secure the feeling with a physical "anchor," some kind of simple signal that represents and triggers the confidence. This

could be holding your thumb between your other thumb and forefinger, touching your ear, or squeezing your wrist.

5. While continuing to feel the confidence and holding this physical anchor, go back again to that experience you identified in step 1, in which confidence would have been a very helpful addition.

6. Watch yourself going through the experience with confidence in place, and see how it changes the situation.

7. Now step inside the situation with the confidence strong (still holding the physical anchor), and go through the experience all over again. Notice how other people respond to you now that you are so confident, and how differently you feel in this setting with your confidence so high.

8. Release the anchor, and count backwards from 73 to 46 by threes.

9. Think of this past experience again, and notice how your memory of it has changed.

10. If you need to strengthen the confidence, go back to step 3 and repeat the process.

11. Now that your confidence is high, think of something you want to do but haven't yet accomplished.

12. In your head, go through that desired future experience with your confidence strong and fully available. Pay careful attention to how everything changes when you approach it from this state of high confidence.

The anchor you established to trigger feelings of confidence can be used any time and in any situation to bring on those feelings and help you operate powerfully and effectively.

Courage and clarity are often masked by fear, feelings of inadequacy, and self-consciousness. Once your confidence has been restored, space is created within you for these other essential qualities to fill.

With clarity regarding what needs to be done, the courage to take action, and the confidence that you can handle whatever comes along, your own precious Bitch is already taking shape.

Another simple way to continue building and strengthening your confidence is to make a list of all the things you've done well and successfully. This is difficult for some women, because they've been taught that giving themselves credit for anything is selfish and boastful. There's a huge difference, however, between boasting and reporting the facts. If a journalist were asked to write about you and what you have done, she would report it all in a factual and honest way without any emotion to cloud or embellish. That's the perspective I'm suggesting as you remember all the things you've proved yourself capable of, things that hint at what you can accomplish in the future. You can begin by starting a list and see what comes up; here's an example:

- My son's school needed $$: I organized a fundraiser, raised $2,000.

- There was an increase in violence against women in the community. I wrote an article for the local paper about the importance of self-defense training. As a result, community leaders offered to sponsor self-defense classes for women and girls.

- My daughter was often sick, and no one could figure out why. I researched chemicals found in household products, and found evidence that the chemicals were the source of her illness. I converted our home to safer products, and Amy got and stayed well.

The point here is to remember the many ways in which you have taken action and created results. Your actions/results list doesn't have to include colossal things like finding a cure for AIDS or coming up with a successful strategy for world peace to be meaningful (although those would be welcome). Any situation in which you have made something worthwhile happen, however small you may think it is, is one more bit of evidence of your power.

Another element of the Bitch's power is motivation. Not only is she aware of what needs to be done in the interest of general well-being, but she has both the courage and the confidence to do it, and she is deeply motivated to take meaningful action. One of the ways she recognizes steps she can take to contribute to the good of all is to measure the level of her motivation. The Bitch is not moved by the "shoulds" that mold the lives of so many; rather she trusts her gut to guide her on the path to meaningful action. If she doesn't feel stimulated or inspired by whatever is presenting itself, she moves on. That doesn't mean that if she doesn't feel like paying her taxes, she just doesn't write that check. Like all of us, there are things she is obligated to do as a responsible member of a community and citizen of the planet. But the Bitch is very discriminating when it comes to causes to be involved in, projects in which to participate, and activities to which she adds her energy and attention.

Also, like all of us, the Bitch can get tired in the course of whatever she's committed to, and can find her motivation flagging. She knows exactly what to do, however, to regain her zeal and enthusiasm for the purpose to which she's dedicated. Remember, it's how you think about something that determines the way you feel about it. When the Bitch finds her zest for something losing steam, she knows that she can consider it in a different way and get re-energized. The following is one way she does it, and you can too. We've touched on this earlier, but it warrants another look:

1. Let an image form in your mind of what you want to accomplish.

2. Add color to the image so that it becomes vibrant.

3. Bring the image closer to you—not so close that it becomes intimidating, but close enough that you could almost reach out and touch it.

4. Make it at least life-sized, perhaps a bit larger than life.

5. Make sure the image is directly in front of you.

6. Add movement to the image. This doesn't have to be radical action, but simply some sort of movement that makes this image more like a movie than a photograph.

7. Add sounds that are motivating, that bring the energy you need to do what you want to do. These sounds could include music, the voice of someone you care for and who believes in you, or any other sounds that pump you up and remind you of just how capable you are.

8. Make sure the image is bright and full of life

9. Notice how you feel as you look at this vibrant, close, larger-than-life, and compelling image.

10. Step into the image, and feel what it's like to be surrounded by its power. As you are in the midst of this exhilarating scene, you may find that you have all the energy you need to take the next step toward the goal.

This simple process is a clear indication of just how powerful your mind is. By simply changing the way you *think* about something, you can quickly change the way you feel. That's pretty remarkable, and it's a great reminder of how important it is to learn to use your mind well, and with integrity. Just as an aside, this process, so effective in increasing motivation and excitement, can also be used to disarm anything that makes you feel anxious or intimidated. Just do it in the reverse: Take the color out of the intimidating image, shrink it down to a much smaller size, move it to one side instead of in front of you, push it farther away, then either take all sound out or add sound that is completely inappropriate to the scene (circus music or the sound of a flushing toilet might work very well). Once you've made those changes, notice how your feelings of anxiety or intimidation have shifted, and how much more in control you feel.

Any of these processes can put you in touch with the power that indicates the presence of your Bitch. When you step into that power and then take action, your results will reflect the virtually unlimited possibilities available to you at this remarkable time of life.

Finding Your Crone

You'll remember that the gifts of the Crone are wisdom and insight. As we've already discussed, the idea of wisdom is often a difficult one to grasp, probably because it seems amorphous, lacking any real shape. The way it gets defined depends on who is doing the defining, and how he or she sees the world. It's a bit like that story of the blind men and the elephant—every definition of wisdom probably holds a piece of the truth. For our purpose here, wisdom is defined as the ability to see beyond the surface to the deeper meaning. It's that ability that makes the Crone the profound being she is.

Remember the young woman I spoke with who thought her college professor was very wise because he knew his field so well? That's a common misunderstanding. As I've already said, wisdom and knowledge are different, and it's important to keep that difference in mind. There are many people who have an impressive amount of knowledge, yet who demonstrate no wisdom at all; and there are others who may have limited formal education and knowledge, but whose lives are shaped by the meaningful insights that characterize the Crone. Consider the wise Crones of fairy tales: Typically, these were women who were not educated in any formal way, but whose connection to and understanding of the natural world and the sacred realm made them founts of insight people couldn't find anywhere else. You have the same capacity for that connection and understanding. As a creation of the Divine, you are a natural vessel for containing and allowing the flow of such sacred information—but you must know how to access that capacity.

We have already touched on a couple of ways to tap into your inner wisdom, but the topic deserves further exploration. First, remember that it's difficult to find that wisdom you carry when your emotions are running the show. As important as it is to recognize and give expression to your feelings, and as much as they can enrich your everyday experience, emotion tends to get in the way when it comes to stepping into the kind of wisdom held by the Crone. When you are attached to a particular outcome, or when insecurities or anxieties are triggered, finding clean and objective insights is unlikely. In order to step into that profound wisdom, it's essential to move beyond emotions that run strong and cloud your perception. As we talked about earlier, the true Crone is most often a serene woman. A major factor in that serenity is her ability to detach from chaotic emotions and understand any situation from a much cleaner place. Keep in mind that this doesn't mean she is unemotional—it means she knows how and when to move beyond emotion to find that deeper perspective.

Years ago I was engaged in an ongoing struggle with a relative whose talent and humor I respected, and whose company I enjoyed. She's a bright, skillful individual whose passion for life occasionally went amok, and who knew exactly how to suck me into her drama. One day she was warm and friendly, the next day she was cold and uncommunicative, and the emotional roller coaster had become difficult for me. On her warm and friendly days, I would feel excited about the connection between us; on her cold and uncommunicative days, I would feel confused and hurt. Eventually the times we spent together devolved into shouting matches and crying jags, and I would come away exhausted and convinced that she and I would always be related by blood, but could never be strong friends. It was just too draining.

One evening, she and I shared a dinner during which I found myself asking her, through gritted teeth and with rage that was only barely contained, "Why are you so mean to me? Why do you hurt me like this? I have always been kind to you, supportive of you; you are such a harsh person, and it's so painful to be around you. Why don't you just go to hell?" It was a terrible evening, and when I got home I felt ashamed of the way I had lashed out at her. It was at that moment that I realized that my agitated response to her was generated by the strong emotion I felt, alternating between positive and negative, toward this woman who was part of my family. I wondered how I might feel if there weren't such a powerful emotional bond between us, and what I might understand about her if I could see her more clearly. My highly emotional reaction to her certainly had no wisdom to it, and only made the situation worse. I needed a way to love and respect her without losing myself in her unpredictable ways.

The pain of this relationship grew out of the fact that I was thoroughly emotionally associated in the situation. That means that I had become far too vulnerable to her ups and downs, and had allowed my sense of self to be deeply affected by her arbitrary behavior and my own disappointed expectation for a stable and consistent friendship. I began practicing dissociation. It took a while to do it well, but the better I got at it, the more I understood, the more compassion I felt, and the less pain I took on. It was a simple exercise, and resulted in a much wiser and more peaceful response to this woman who had been a source of such confusion and anger. As long as I had been so emotionally attached, I couldn't see her clearly, and I could only react with strong feelings. Finding a way to detach just enough to see what was really happening between us gave me more options in my response. This same exercise can allow you to step back emotionally from a person or a situation when your response leaves you less resourceful than you want to be. This can be a huge step toward uncovering the wisdom that lies within you.

The process is very simple, only takes a few minutes, and can be done anywhere. It's useful both with feelings that come up as you relive a situation from the past that continues to haunt you, and with current situations that bring up the strong emotions that can get in the way of wisdom. It goes like this:

1. Allow an image of the troubling event to come to mind. If the situation is something that's going on currently, you can use this process at the very moment it's occurring.

2. Notice how you feel as you either remember what happened or experience it in the moment. Pay attention to how you feel about yourself and the other person/people in the experience.

3. Now, leaving your body in whatever is going on, allow your mind to drift up to a spot above the situation, perhaps about ceiling level—still close enough to see and hear the details, but no longer engaged in the circumstance. From this location you can be aware of much more than you were when in the thick of things.

4. Having taken this somewhat removed and much more objective position, watch and listen for a moment to everything that's happening in the situation you just floated out of. You are now observing yourself and everyone else involved, as if they were strangers and you were simply passing by and pausing for a moment to watch the show.

5. As the neutral observer with no attachment to anyone involved, allow yourself to notice the things you couldn't pick up on when you were in the midst of the situation. From here you might see how something the other person does triggers a reaction that is out of proportion reaction, or how your gestures and facial expression serve to increase the other person's upset, and therefore accelerate the emotional downward spiral between you. From this slightly detached position, you can also hear how your tone of voice may sound condescending, or how the other individual's sarcasm leaves you feeling dismissed and devalued.

6. Having noticed the details that escaped you in the heat of the moment, you can now make new choices regarding the way you relate to and communicate with anyone who is/was part of this event. You can't control what the others do, but you can, and must, choose to control the way you conduct yourself in similar circumstances. When you choose to change, everyone else involved will change to adjust to your new behavior and attitude. As a result, the outcome of the situation will be different.

As this process indicates, much of the wisdom of the Crone comes from her ability and willingness to see the big picture in any circumstance, instead of getting trapped in and limited by a single perception. If she chooses only to see life through a lens made up of her own feelings, biases, and fears, her world will stay small. By opting to understand the viewpoint and experience of others, she ensures that her own experience will be vast, profound, and multi-layered.

Earlier in the book, I also mentioned another way the Crone learned to allow her wisdom to emerge. This has to do with exploring all possible angles of a situation before deciding how to respond. In her days B.W. (Before Wisdom), the Crone, like most of us, based her response in any situation on her strongest and most immediate emotion. She often took things personally that in truth had nothing to do with her, and was frequently in a state of high vigilance, always ready to defend herself or to accept someone else's idea of truth and deny her own. Upon discovering wisdom, however, she realized that she can acknowledge her initial response, and then put it aside for a moment while she examines the myriad interpretations that might apply. This gives her the opportunity to respond more resourcefully than that initial emotion might have allowed. This doesn't mean that if she sees a child about to run into the path of an oncoming car, she takes a moment to explore the possible meanings of such behavior. She knows the difference between the situations that require immediate action, and those in which a deeper look would be a good idea. As I said before, the guy who cuts her off in traffic might be an inconsiderate creep, or he may be rushing to the hospital because a loved one has been in an accident. Each of those possibilities evokes a different response. One is probably more productive than the other.

Questions that help the Crone expand her perspective in any situation include:

- What else might this circumstance mean?
- What would the behavior I'm observing mean if *I* were doing it?
- What could be motivating this person to take such action?
- What do I see of myself in this other person's actions?
- How can I make a positive difference here?

These questions are not intended to excuse inappropriate behavior, but rather to create space within which to interpret and understand things differently, and maybe more accurately. True wisdom is vast, and the Crone is characterized by such vastness. There is plenty of space in her heart and spirit for compassion and forgiveness.

Earlier, I shared a story about a client whose brother had been a source of pain and confusion since they were kids. The process we used to assist my client in moving out of that pain and into an unexpected kind of compassion and forgiveness is another one that can provide a giant leap toward the full-blown wisdom of which you are capable. As we've seen, choosing to hold on to pain rather than forgive ensures that true wisdom will remain beyond your grasp. The process that helped my client understand and forgive the brother who had been so difficult provides the opportunity to step into someone else's world long enough to see life through his or her eyes, and to understand his or her behaviors in a whole new way. This is another simple yet meaningful way to move beyond limitation and into wisdom. You can do this by yourself or with the help of a trusted friend. The steps are as follows:

1. Pick out three spots on the floor, one for you, one for the person you haven't yet been able to forgive, and one for the neutral observer.

2. Stand in your spot, looking toward the other person's position. As you imagine seeing the other person standing in his or her spot, express out loud whatever you need to say, and describe what you feel regarding the person you need to forgive.

3. When you've finished, recite out loud the ten last letters in the alphabet, beginning with Z and going backwards (Z, Y, X, W, and so on).

4. Now move to the spot that represents the person who remains unforgiven. Step onto that spot, and take a moment to become that other person. You won't be there for long, so don't be concerned about getting stuck. Take as long as you need to move deeply into what life is like for that person, taking into account everything you know about his situation: his pain, loss, hopes, loneliness, fear, family situation ... Imagine that you have become him, and are feeling everything that makes up his experience.

5. As this other person, look at the spot you just moved from and see yourself there, but through the eyes of this other individual you have stepped into.

6. As the person you need to forgive, say whatever you need to say and describe what you are feeling. Remember, you are doing this as the other person, not as yourself.

7. When you're done, quickly name five state capitals starting with the letter B, and then return to your original spot on the floor.

8. Back in your own spot, having experienced what it's like to be this other individual, notice how your feelings toward him or her have shifted.

9. Now move to the neutral observer position, and from that uninvolved place express whatever you observe about the other two individuals and their behavior toward each other.

10. Finally, move back into your own spot, bringing with you the objective impressions of the neutral observer. Pulling all this information together, you will likely find that the negative feelings you've been carrying toward the other person have changed, perhaps dramatically. Forgiveness now becomes a natural and even comfort-able act.

These two processes are very effective for unraveling emotional entanglements and releasing negative and taxing feelings that have prevented you from discovering your inherent wisdom. Forgiveness and compassion open the door to a deeper realm, and the Crone makes a habit of them.

The true foundation for the kind of wisdom that transcends intellectual understanding, however, is found in relationship to the Divine. Since Spirit is the Source of all life and all wisdom, it makes sense that the more deeply connected to this Source we choose to be, the more of Its wisdom we will contain. Now, if each of us carries the spark of the Divine within, then what do I mean when I suggest that we be "deeply connected"? If I carry it, I'm already connected, right? Certainly; however, if we carry that divine spark and are not aware of it, we aren't reaping the benefits of our own divine nature and the sacredness of life. So, I'm suggesting that we choose to become more conscious of the presence of God in and around us, and more open and receptive to that sacred wisdom.

The Crones I know and have worked with share a powerful desire to live as conduits for the wisdom of God. Because of their commitment to serve as expressions of the Divine on earth, they have learned to choose their responses and actions carefully. Questions like "How can I best demonstrate the love of the Divine in this situation?" help shape the way they live. "Love the planet and all its inhabitants through me" is their constant request, and their immediate response to any circumstance is to find evidence of the sacred therein. Consistently willing to see others through the eyes of God, these are remarkable women. What makes them remarkable is their willingness to put ego aside and to serve as channels for what is often called the All That Is. By trying the processes detailed above, and by asking yourself the questions listed as you begin each day, you will find your own exquisite openness, and the wisdom you carry will begin to present itself.

Finding Your Harlot

Finding your Harlot requires paying attention in ways that may be new to you. The gifts of this sensual woman are passion and awareness, and her commitment is to have plenty of both. Let me repeat something I've already said—the Harlot is not a hedonist. This is not a woman whose *raison d'être* is to live a self-serving existence in which pleasure is the only goal. But the Harlot has recognized that there is a constant stream of information coming at her through her senses, and that if she isn't attentive she'll miss much of the richness her life could hold. This woman is not willing to miss out on anything that speaks to the lushness of a life fully informed.

Many people, maybe most, spend the bulk of their time in a state of preoccupation. Their energy and focus tend to be split among regret or nostalgia for the past, fear or anticipation of the future, and just enough for the present moment to avoid being run over by that truck they didn't see because they were too busy thinking about something else. As we've already seen, this is an unfortunate way to live because it doesn't allow for a full experience of the present moment. The Harlot has learned this lesson, and knows that a rich, full life is lived with senses wide open. She also recognizes that there is no need to manufacture sensual experiences that may be contrived at best, and dangerous at worst, because life, when one participates fully, fairly oozes sensual information. If one's senses are not stimulated, one simply isn't paying attention.

There are five basic senses through which we gain information, and they are the only ways we can know anything at all. We've said it before: We either see, hear, feel, taste, or smell, and if any or all of those channels are limited in what they allow in, we are only partially informed. Being only partially informed means being only partially alive and having only partial joy, abundance, success, and love.

Just like all your other muscles, your senses need to be exercised in order to function at their peak. So many of us are used to just skimming across the surface of our experiences, unaware of just how unaware we are. So, if I don't know how much I don't know, how can I begin expanding the range of information I take in? The key is to pay attention in new ways, and to regard every kind of sensual impression as having value.

Your senses are also called "sensory modalities," and they include the visual, auditory, kinesthetic, gustatory, and olfactory. Each of these modalities has distinct qualities or smaller elements that enrich sensory experiences. Once you know what those submodalities are, you can, with intention, begin to exercise those sensory muscles and build your internal database of information.

Let's begin with a description of the submodalities that pertain to each of your senses:

VISUAL

- Location—Is it in front of you, above or below, or off to one side?

- Distance—How close to you is it?

- Brightness—Is it light and bright, or dark and somber?

- Shape

- Color or black and white?

- Form—Is it all around you (panoramic) or a separate image caught in a frame?

- Transparent or opaque?

- Vivid or muted?

- Horizontal or vertical?

- Size

- Three-dimensional or flat?

By noticing each of these qualities separately, and then noticing how these qualities combine (color and shape, for instance, or size and location), your visual sense gets stronger, and you become more aware. Remember, the point here is not to come to some conclusion about what you're seeing, but rather to get used to paying better and more detailed attention to the world around you. Here's an example: I was walking in my neighborhood recently, and I found a small flower bed in which several kinds of flowers were beginning to bloom. I noticed in particular poppies and irises. As I bent down to get a closer look, I realized that the round pods that hold the poppy blossoms are covered with fuzz that matches the fuzz on the leaves. The iris blossoms, however, are contained in pods that are smooth and more rectangular and pointed than the poppy pods. The poppies were beginning to bloom in vibrant orange, while the irises were starting to show themselves in various shades of purple and gold.

Now, is this life-changing information? Probably not; however, the visual impressions of such beauty and complexity had an impact on me, shifting my state of mind. I could have moved right past them, caught up in whatever was going on in my head, and missed the vibrant colors, the intricate shapes, the evidence of both diversity and harmony found consistently in nature. Simply by choosing to look for things of visual interest, I got a big boost in both my outlook and my energy. I had begun that walk with the intention to find indications of spring, and they were everywhere. Had I not been looking for them, open to their subtle impact, I would probably have missed them—and missed out on the effect their unique beauty had on the way I felt and the way I noticed other things during the rest of that day.

AUDITORY

- Location

- Tone

- Tempo

- Volume

- Rhythm

- Source—Is the sound external or internal to you?

- Distance

- Stereo or monaural?

- Timbre

- One sound or many?

- Continuous or pulsating?

- Melody

- Resonant or dissonant?

Sound is so powerful that it can often generate images and feelings. Because the majority of people tend to be highly visual (taking in information primarily through what they see), sound is frequently relegated to the background of any experience they may be having. But when they become aware of the multitude of sounds happening all around them most of the time, they begin to recognize how powerful the auditory sense can be. Early in the morning, I can hear at least seven or eight different bird songs while sitting on my deck. If I walk to the park at that same time of day, there are closer to a dozen distinct songs available. When I was younger, I didn't notice these things. They just didn't seem important in the scope of everything I had going on. Now, however, I find that they bring with them a feeling of peace and another kind of beauty for me to perceive and take in. Somehow, being aware of the sounds around me and of what they imply about human experience helps put things in balance. Whatever is going on in my life is less likely to pull me off track when I am reminded of the harmony and balance in the natural world. I'm not sure I can explain it well—it's as if sound helps me remember that my experiences are parts of a much larger fabric, that the flow of life and harmony in nature has been constant since the beginning, and will continue to be constant no matter what I am experiencing. Somehow, I find that comforting.

Think about all the different sounds you can make with your own voice. It's amazing, really. There is so much you can discern just from the tone and timbre of a person's voice. I remember a situation in which I knew from the sound of my boyfriend's voice that he was about to leave the relationship. The stress he was feeling as he prepared to leave was evident in the sound of his voice. And consider how many kinds of music there are in the world, and the fact that they all make use of the virtually unlimited range of sounds present in life. Sound is everywhere, and an incredible amount of information is presented auditorily. Try this: Go for a walk with the goal of noticing how many different sounds you hear. Make a list so later you can count the multitude of sounds that make up your day-to-day experience. The more you hear, the more you know.

KINESTHETIC

- Pressure
- Location
- Texture
- Temperature
- Movement
- Intensity
- Weight

Additionally, the kinesthetic, or feeling, modality can be divided into three separate areas:

- Tactile—The skin senses

- Proprioceptive—Muscular and other internal sensations

- Evaluative meta-feelings—Feelings about other perceptions or representations, which generally show up as emotions

The Harlot is familiar with all of them, and trusts her kinesthetic sense to alert her to things that need her attention, and to confirm what her other senses have told her. Have you ever been in a situation in which something just didn't feel right, and your decision to keep your distance later proved to be the best one? Have you learned to "trust your gut" when facing a choice or course of action? Much of this kind of guidance involves your kinesthetic sense, and the Harlot knows how important it is to honor and respect this source of sensory direction.

And what about sex? Can you imagine how many of us would quickly lose interest if our kinesthetic sense weren't functioning well? By being open to physical sensations and the information they communicate, the Harlot has the opportunity to understand more about herself and others, and to forge bonds that can bear fruit on several levels.

The Harlot's tendency toward the physical can set her apart from those who are uncomfortable with touch and physical connection in general. She may touch others as she speaks, may hug someone she's just been introduced to, and may be the first to offer a physical expression of comfort to someone in pain. This inclination to respond physically has nothing to do with her sexuality, but rather demonstrates that the Harlot gathers information and understands her world through her senses.

The Harlot is as alert to her senses of taste and smell as she is the others, regularly picking up on fragrances and flavors others, too distracted to notice, have missed. Words that occur to her as she tastes and smells her way through life include stale, fresh, floral, smoky, citrus, earthy, sour, sweet, salty, juicy ...

I once taught a workshop designed to help increase sensory awareness, and to assist women in recognizing the sensuality they carry. At one point, while exploring taste and smell, I provided a number of items with distinctive flavors or fragrances, and asked the participants, eyes closed, to identify each item by tasting or smelling. People were amazed at what they experienced: Without the visual or tactile information they were used to, they were able to be more aware than ever of the tastes and smells of the items provided. Because of that focus, their experience of each was stronger and more defined.

So, here's the point: By choosing to pay better attention to the information coming to you through your senses, you are choosing to become better informed. You are opting not only to take all that information in, but also to use it to expand your own world, to add it all to the mix, and to come up with a life that is richer, more textured, and multi-layered in a way that serves you instead of draining you dry.

You may already have lots of ideas for strengthening your senses. Here are a few more:

- Take a walk along same route for several days in a row. Each day, choose one of your senses to concentrate on, and then pay close attention to everything you notice through the Sense of the Day.

- For many people, the sense of smell is a strong evoker of memories. Try this: Pick out several things that have strong fragrances (or odors) and notice what pictures or memories come to mind as you smell each of them. The senses are interwoven, and smell often activates the others.

- Try touching someone you love in a way that is different than usual, and notice how each of you responds. Pay attention to how the skin on one part of his or her body feels as compared to how it feels on another area. Notice the difference between stroking skin and stroking hair. How do smells enhance your experience in an intimate setting?

The Harlot is constantly being informed by her senses. She uses that information to make sense of her experience and to find the personal rhythm that allows her to move in sync with the earth and with Source. Hers is a well-informed life, one fed by an inexhaustible well of joy. She has learned to live an important lesson, that if she excites her senses in any manner of ways, she will, as a result, renew her spirit.

The power of sensory awareness must also be considered in the area of education, if we are to teach our children well. By training students to ignore the information available through the senses, we cripple them and doom them to lives of narrow and limited experience. Writer David Polis has expressed this well: "Must we always teach our children with books? Let them look at the stars and the mountains above. Let them look at the waters and the trees and flowers on earth. Then they will begin to think, and to think is the beginning of a real education."

Ronald Kotulak, science writer for the *Chicago Tribune,* was also aware of the connection between the senses and a deeper kind of education. He observed that ...

By pushing the right biological buttons in the brain, scientists are finding they can make the future brighter for many children whose development otherwise would have been stunted ... How the buttons work is perhaps the most amazing things of all. The buttons are the senses: vision, taste, smell, touch and sound, and they can be pushed by experiences from the outside world.

As I sit writing early in the morning, I notice a window washer on a platform midway up a high-rise building across the street. The rising sun throws shadows of the long ropes holding his platform across the face of the building. As the ropes sway, the huge shadows dance gracefully along the entire height of the building. It is a simple thing, but as I watch I am captivated by the beauty of the scene. Would I have even noticed this when I was younger? Perhaps, but not with the same degree of awe I have now. Life has brought me to a place from which I notice things I missed earlier. It is only now, with half of life under my belt, that I am equipped to understand the power of the sensuous realm.

5

Bringing Your Gifts
to the World

Who are we at the midpoint of our lives? We are not who we used to be only older. In truth, we are much more. Consider the chrysalis, caterpillar, and butterfly: The caterpillar doesn't go into the chrysalis, hang out for a while, and then emerge the same as he used to be, only looking older and a bit more worn. He comes out as an entirely different being. The same can be true for all of us as we move into the chrysalis that transitions us into middle age. What is required of us, if we are to complete the process with grace, is to be willing to let go of our old idea of who we are. That doesn't mean letting go of the things that have been meaningful in the first half of life; it means allowing ourselves the flexibility to shift our emotional shape and become an expanded and deeper version of who we are.

Transformation doesn't mean suddenly going from stay-at-home mom to aggressive career woman; nor does it mean moving from assertive professional to stay-at-home needlepointer. It means moving your point of reference from the external to the internal, and recognizing that you contain all you need to step into a profound experience of an expanded self. It means assimilating all you've learned about yourself and about life, and taking it to the deeper level that becomes available to us at the midpoint of our lives. The early part of our lives is often externally focused, as we have seen. Entering midlife with that same external focus ensures that this process of transformation will be more challenging and frustrating than it needs to be. Hanging on white-knuckled to the idea of who we were earlier, and insisting on remaining that person even though it no longer works, can make midlife more painful and confusing than it is intended to be. On the other hand, entering midlife with anticipation and an eye to a whole new world of possibility will ensure that the next part of your life won't be a route leading to the end, but rather a pathway to a deeper place than you may ever have imagined. Middle age isn't just a matter of aging. When entered into full bore and fully aware, it is the process and result of true transformation.

As a girl, I heard a lot about The Change in conversations that usually carried the impression that this mysterious event was something to dread. "Are you going through The Change?" women of a certain age were asked in a whisper, as if the whole thing was shameful. "Oh, you'll get there one day. You'll know how hard life is when you go through The Change." This was something I heard more than once from women who were older than I was. The Change was clearly unavoidable, negative, painful, and the final mile marker before the grave. But I have found it to be something different.

I suppose that when women refer to the change of life, they're speaking mostly of menopause—and I'll admit that hot flashes, night sweats, mood swings, insomnia, and the general drying out that seems to be an integral part of the process are all in the Inconvenient Occurrences category, at least for me. And sometimes they move in a harsh and disrespectful way to the Pain in the Butt category. But these things are temporary; they come and go while we're in the throes of menopause, and then eventually they're over and life goes on. For women who are perimenopausal (not in menopause yet but heading in that direction), the fearful anticipation of these shifts, often based on horror stories they've heard from others, can set them up to make middle age exactly what they're afraid it will be. I have worked with many women who, without even realizing it, just slid right into what everyone had told them middle age would be like. They molded themselves and their experience to fit the generally accepted perception of middle-aged women, instead of shaping society's perception to fit who they were becoming.

Your response to living from the midpoint of your life and beyond is determined by what you choose to focus on. Sure, midlife is a time of change, but what time of life isn't? Every period of your life has brought change, has required adjustment, and has shown you new things. Middle age is no different. Focus on the aspects of this part of your life that you deem negative, or spend your time and energy grieving whatever elements of youth you think are lost to you, and you will miss the power, the wisdom, and the sensuality that midlife is meant to express. Focus on the profound and life-changing aspects of being middle-aged, and your Bitch, Crone, and Harlot will emerge gladly.

Have I told you about the changes I went through as I headed into my own midlife experience? In the beginning it was rough, and it stayed rough until I realized that I could make it something else. My body began to change in ways I didn't appreciate, men weren't looking at me the way they used to, my libido appeared to be on hiatus, and my sense of purpose seemed to vanish. And people started calling me "Ma'am". I came face to face with the fact that I had lived half of my life basing my sense of who I was on the responses I got from other people, and I wasn't enjoying the changes in those responses. I had three distinct options: I could pretend I was still who I was at age thirty (no one would be fooled) and come across as a pathetic and desperate middle-aged woman; I could get bitter and depressed about half of my life being over; or I could re-define myself and form the second half of life around the depth of things I had learned and had to offer. Only one of those options brought with it the possibility of joy .... and it was high time for joy.

Re-definition is in the air for those of us who aren't willing to do middle age the way our grandmothers (or mothers) did it. We all know lots of people who are eager to define us—to tell us how we should live, who we should be, and what's appropriate for us. But when you find the courage to crawl out from under the weight of all those definitions and begin creating your own, life can become very interesting indeed.

You can begin by gathering up all the definitions of you that have been offered by others over the years, examining them carefully and with great honesty, selecting those that really fit the person who's been living inside you all this time, and gently and respectfully discarding the others. With all those mistaken impressions out of the way, you are free to re-think yourself and come up with a more fitting idea of who you are at the midpoint of your life. Or maybe you don't want to define yourself at all; maybe it's time to live spontaneously, trying new things, going new places, all the while learning more about what is possible and what doesn't fit for you. The point is to begin thinking about yourself and about middle age in ways—maybe new ways—that serve and enrich you. It doesn't matter how the second half of life has been for others; it can be different, better, more meaningful for you.

Recently, I heard an interview with a very successful actress in her sixties. She made the statement that she is now in the "final act" of her life, and that she is winding down as she prepares for the end. I don't choose to look at my life that way. Is life a process with a beginning, middle, and end? Sure. Even if you subscribe to the concept of reincarnation, each lifetime has its own stages, and eventually comes to an end. Am I aware that at some point life as I know it will end? Of course. However, I find no value in making that end my focus. Every day I wake up still breathing is a day in which I can explore more of the richness life offers. Being excited about uncovering more of life's treasures requires the curiosity and wonder we've already talked about. I'm not sure how possible it is to maintain that inquisitive approach, that awe and wonder about life, if we've chosen to think of ourselves as beings for whom the good and powerful stuff is pretty much over, and who are now tasked with preparing for the ultimate checkout. Every moment of our lives can be touched with awe. If we are not in awe, we aren't paying attention.

Most of us spent the first half of life scrambling to fit the criteria, the requirements of a society focused on things like physical beauty, sex, money, and influence. At the midpoint, however, it's time to take a long, hard look at those requirements. A big piece of thinking differently about being middle-aged has to do with coming up with your own criteria. What makes life really meaningful to you at this point? What is most important to you at this juncture? Kindness? Creativity? Honesty? Affection? Making a difference in the world? Taking more risks? The things that are paramount for you now help form the criteria by which you can assess success, reward, meaning, and purpose during this new stage of life. For instance, I have very different friends now than I did when I was younger. I look for different qualities now than I used to, and I have come to understand that I am most comfortable with people who share my love of the earth and nature, and who are truly wise, spiritual, and compassionate individuals. Earlier in life my criteria for people with whom I formed friendships included things like popularity, coolness, fashion sense, and influence. Now, there's nothing wrong with those things; they just aren't as important to me any more. My criteria have changed as I have changed. Establishing my own idea about making life meaningful has allowed me to make choices that are honest and that work for me as I am right now. You get to form your own criteria for a life well lived, and you aren't bound by what others find important.

When you were younger, you probably set goals for yourself. And you may have accomplished many, maybe even most, of them. But what about now? Early in life, goals feel important because they are milestones by which we can measure our progress. But I often find that as women hit midlife, they tend to lose sight of the power of goals. It's almost as if there's nothing more to work toward, so goals are irrelevant. Those who have discovered their Bitch, Crone, and Harlot, however, tend to live vibrant lives filled with strategies for expanding their worlds even further. This means goals, whether big or small, play an essential part in how these emotionally and spiritually larger-than-life women approach everything they do. The kind of goals you set isn't the point here; the important thing is that you set goals, that you establish intentions for yourself that keep you moving toward an ever increasing awareness of the infinite magic that fills you.

Maybe you want to continue your education, or perhaps you've always wanted to learn to belly dance. You might move to a foreign location, or decide to learn a faux painting technique so you can change the look of your home. It's all good, and one goal will lead to the next. This will keep you in a state of forward momentum, and life will begin to feel like a treasure hunt. What interests you? What have you thought about doing, but never got around to? By setting goals for yourself, goals that can both nurture and comfort, you ensure that there is always a direction in which to channel your energy. With that can come a renewed sense of purpose.

You are in a position to be a significant role model for younger women for whom the whole idea of being middle-aged is murky at best, and for other middle-aged women whose sense of themselves is keeping them stuck in feelings and behaviors that don't begin to express who they are truly meant to be. By choosing to step outside the tight and constricting little box middle age is often thought to be—or if you like the structure a box provides, by simply expanding the walls—you become a trailblazer, one who demonstrates a different and more rewarding way to live the second half of life. Those observing you as you express your Bitch, Crone, and Harlot in your everyday life will be able to create a much vaster and grander vision of what women are capable of after spending half a life learning, growing, and refining the gifts that are inherent in them.

So, where should you begin in this process of revealing the power, wisdom, and sensuality you have been accumulating? Should you be the Bitch, or the Crone, or the Harlot? The answer is that we need to be all three. Developing one or even two of these archetypes ensures a life lived out of balance. It is in the emerging of all three of these aspects of ourselves that we become fully alive, fully present, and fully impossible to ignore. Each of them informs the others, and without all three present, our experience is incomplete. Without the wisdom of the Crone, the Bitch may take a lot of action and create many outcomes, but they may not be the best actions or the most useful outcomes. Without the sensory information of the Harlot, the Crone's insights are limited and her wisdom imperfect. Without the power of the Bitch, the Harlot takes in a lot of valuable information, but can't use it to take meaningful action.

As stated earlier, you carry the seeds of each of these archetypes. They are all available to you, but you can begin by recognizing which of the three is most evident in you already. And remember that gratitude is in order when you find something so significant already operating within yourself. The next step is to strengthen the others: Try using the processes detailed earlier, and begin paying careful attention to the evidence of all three in your life. Not only will you begin to feel differently about yourself and this time in your life, but you will also notice that others respond differently to you as they recognize the power, wisdom, and sensuality you carry.

You may, on occasion, find yourself understanding something in a way that is limited to one or the other of these archetypes. If, for instance, you are reacting to something strictly from the perspective of the Bitch, wanting to take action and make things happen in the situation, pause for a moment and ask yourself how the Crone or the Harlot might operate in that same circumstance. Move for a moment out of the Bitch position, and into the position of the Crone, looking at the situation through the eyes of her wisdom, or into the perspective of the Harlot, from which you can notice through your senses a great deal more information about what's really going on. Taking a minute to experience things from all three positions can ensure that any action you take will be well informed and bring about the highest quality results.

We've talked about the Change of Life, and how it's perceived by many as an indication that we're wrapping things up and on our way out. That is, as we have seen, total nonsense. The real Change of Life, the one that deserves our attention and commitment, goes deeper than shifts in hormone levels and the end of our childbearing years. This is the Change that offers you the opportunity to become and express the extraordinary woman you are intended to be, and puts you in the Wise and Revered Elder category. This is the Change that takes you from other people's expectations and into the dazzling experience of honoring yourself. This is the Change that provides the power, wisdom, and sensuality to create the life you may only have hoped was possible. This is the Change characterized by the following:

- You know more now than you have ever known. As a result you have more to offer than ever before.

- You have a history of making things happen, big and small.

- You have successfully dealt with numerous challenges.

- You have proven that you can deal with whatever comes along.

- You have more experience than ever, and more than anyone younger.

- Whether you realize it or not, because of your experience, you have amassed a great deal of wisdom and learned different ways of looking at and understanding things.

- You may know more than ever before about what you want.

- You probably aren't nearly as concerned about what people think as when you were younger, and not as eager for their approval. That means you are freer than before.

- You are free to express your sensuality in new ways, without the agendas sensuality and sexuality carried in your youth. You now have the option of embodying more authentic sensual and sexual power.

- You are most likely clearer about what works and doesn't work for you in a relationship.

- You may feel more willing to ask for what you need.

This is a pretty impressive list, and most if not all of the items apply to you—you just may not realize it. By working with your Bitch, Crone, and Harlot, anything on the list that you'd like to develop further will get stronger. It's up to you to regard yourself in light of everything you have to offer, and everything you're capable of. It's all in there, and it's time to call it forth.

And, by the way, just in case you've been told that you should expect memory problems and fuzzy thinking because you're middle-aged or older, there's an article called "The Surprising Power of the Aging Brain" in which the statements are made that "more and more neurologists and psychologists are coming to the conclusion that the brain at midlife—a period increasingly defined as the years from thirty-five to sixty-five and even beyond—is a much more elastic, much more supple thing than anyone ever realized," and "for many people the aging process not only does not batter the brain, it actually makes it better."[1]

Imagine a world in which every woman has discovered her power, wisdom, and sensuality and is using them for the benefit of all life and the planet itself. Imagine a planet on which women understand and support each other and come together to achieve the well-being we all want—the abundance, joy, health, safety, security, love, respect, fun, and spiritual awareness that lead to a life worth waking up to. I recently read something actress Meg Ryan said as she traveled to various third-world locations. As she met women who, in many cases, were living in very difficult circumstances, she observed that "if you empower women, you can change the world."

At midlife, because we have learned so much and have so much experience, I believe we can say it a little differently: *When women empower themselves, they can change the world.* I don't think this is an overstatement. Sometimes when I'm out in public observing women and all they can accomplish, I wonder what our planet and our species would be like if women were committed to each other and to achieving the critical mass that could bring peace, health, and safety to all. As we move into the midpoint of our lives and beyond, there is something we all must remember: Not only are we the glue that holds everything together, we are, especially at this period of power, wisdom, and sensuality, the force that can transform the world. Transformation and healing of our planet won't happen through military action or political power. It will happen through the critical mass created by women, many of them middle-aged and older, who are committed to living with spiritual wisdom and honoring all of life.

So here we are, having been through the joyful wringer that is the first half of life—and having, in the process, gathered everything we need to make things happen, to move through life with unparalleled wisdom, and to find wonder and delight in every sensuous moment. We know more now than we have ever known, and have the possibility of making life a greater adventure than we had ever imagined. The question now becomes, what will we do with all we have gained? The answer, I believe, lies in a story about the Sufi poet Rumi and his friend, Shams of Tabriz. It is said that Shams took all of Rumi's books and threw them in a fishpond. "Now," he said to the startled Rumi, "you must live what you know." And so it is for each of us.

6

Honoring (and Becoming) the Archetypes in Our Lives

I t's often easy to recognize the powerful, wise, and sensual women who have made their fortunes and become celebrated members of our world. But what about the everyday women who are constantly demonstrating the Bitch, Crone, and Harlot energies they have cultivated and refined? They are all around us, and deserve our appreciation and respect. These are living, breathing examples of what women are capable of when they pull to the surface the power, wisdom, and sensuality they carry, and apply them to day-to-day situations. These are women who are changing the world, in both big and small ways. These women hold up the mirror for the rest of us, and quietly urge us to become everything we are meant to be. The following are examples of the well-known and not-so-well-known women who live their power, wisdom, and sensuality, and in the process enhance life for all of us. You'll find that more than one of the archetypes we've explored show up in each of these women. Ideally, there is overlap of the three in those women who have discovered and are revealing their deeper nature. Remember, they serve as examples of what is possible for every woman who chooses to live a life of excellence, no matter who she is.

WOMEN OF WISDOM

Maya Angelou

America's most well respected poet didn't achieve her status easily. Her childhood was shaped by poverty, separation from her parents, a rape at the age of eight, and the ruthless discrimination rampant in the American South during the 1930s and 1940s. At sixteen, she bore a child and faced the stigma of being an unmarried teenager. She later dabbled in drugs to escape the despair that filled her life, and prostitution in an attempt to support herself and her son.

After returning to dance as an outlet, she was offered an opportunity to tour with the company of *Porgy and Bess,* and to perform in the musical all over the world. In the process, her own political and spiritual horizons began expanding, and her interest in the growing civil rights movement increased. In the 1960s, Dr. Martin Luther King, Jr. asked Maya to coordinate his organization's activities in northern cities, and she was quickly thrust to the forefront of the movement. During this time she married a South African activist, moved to north Africa, and worked in several locations, writing and giving a voice to the people.

After returning to the States, Maya wrote numerous books about her life, including her first book, *I Know Why the Caged Bird Sings,* which tells of the trauma of her early rape, the violent death of her attacker, and her subsequent refusal to speak for five years. Her other works detail the struggles of African-American women, and issues like discrimination, exploitation, and conflict. In spite of the nature of her topics, Maya Angelou's work offers a hopeful, proud, and tenacious perspective that reflects her own dogged determination to survive, and then to thrive.

The list of her work is impressive and diverse—including autobiographies, poetry, plays, children's books, screenplays, recordings, and various film and television appearances—and her credentials impeccable. Besides numerous honorary degrees from prestigious universities and colleges, she has received a Pulitzer Prize nomination for her book *Just Give Me a Cool Drink of Water 'Fore I Die* (1972), a Grammy for Best Spoken Word Album (1994), several Distinguished Service awards, the Lifetime Achievement Award for Literature (1999), and was named one of the top 100 Best Writers of the Twentieth Century by Writer's Digest (1999). She was also selected to compose and deliver an original poem at the inauguration of President Bill Clinton in 1993, and in 2000 was awarded the Presidential Medal of Arts by then President Clinton.

The life of this profoundly wise renaissance woman reflects the theme central to all her work: that the human spirit is able to address and triumph over whatever challenges life offers. She is living proof.

Sarasvati Buhrman, Ph.D.

Outside, on the streets of a bustling college town, it is noisy, crowded, and chaotic; but in the office of Dr. Sarasvati Buhrman, peace and tranquility prevail. The glow about this intriguing woman seems to imply that she knows things of an eternal nature, things others may not be aware of.

Sarasvati Buhrman is a yogic nun. No shaved head or saffron robes, no nun's habit or solemn demeanor; she is, rather, a bright and vibrant woman whose eyes speak volumes about the serenity she's found. Her lifelong practice of yoga has shaped both her work and her personal life in profound ways. "Yoga reveals the divine spark in all of us," she says. Her own divine spark seems to fill whatever space she is in, and is evident is all she does.

A painful childhood, combined with negative news bombarding her from the media, made Sarasvati deeply aware of the pain in the world, and led her to question the concept of a loving God presented in her Christian upbringing. "I couldn't come to terms with the idea of an omnipotent and loving deity who would at the same time allow such pain," she remembers. "I figured that if there is a God, we must be of a very different nature." But even in the face of her skepticism about religion and what she found to be its contradictions, Dr. Buhrman remained intrigued with life, consciousness, and the study of how living things work. That interest motivated her  to undergraduate work in biology, and, much later, doctoral studies in psychological anthropology. But it was early in her academic career, in 1973, while a graduate student in genetics, that everything changed.

"It was just an average morning, when I awoke suddenly with a powerful thought ringing in my head: 'What are you doing?' I heard. 'Have you forgotten everything? You're supposed to be meditating'. I knew nothing of yoga and almost nothing about meditation—only that the Beatles had gone to India to study meditation with some teacher. The only meditation teaching I could find in my local area at the time was Transcendental Meditation (a simple mantra practice), and I began to do it daily."

In 1974 she moved to California, where she learned to meditate on the chakras, the body's subtle energy centers, which brought about a considerable deepening of her practice. In 1976, she met Baba Hari Dass, a monk who taught her yoga philosophy and techniques in the kind of authentic detail she had never known existed. He also introduced her to Ayurvedic medicine (an ancient holistic system of healing practiced in India that seeks to heal the fragmentation and disorder of the mind-body complex and restore wholeness and harmony). Under his guidance she began to understand life, its source, and the healing power of connection to the Divine.

From there, through intense study of the rich connection between two profound and ancient disciplines, Yoga and Ayurveda, she chose to take the vows of a yogic nun, and to spend her life teaching and counseling those seeking healing or spiritual growth through integration of body, mind, and spirit.

Sarasvati's life and work are based on an inner drive for the spiritual, and that drive shapes the way she lives. "There are four kinds of people who come to the spiritual life," she explains. "Some are drawn to God because of great pain in their lives, while others long for knowledge of higher things. The third group of people who seek God are those who simply want a better earthly experience; and the fourth are those who already have deep experiential knowledge of the Divine, and will complete their spiritual journey in this lifetime. I belong to the second group, but I have also had much experience of the first."

Dr. Buhrman defines wisdom as "occurring in stages of enlightenment that help us know the difference between the permanent and the impermanent, the important and the unimportant in life." That understanding begins with the desire to know a higher reality or to develop virtues such as goodness and selflessness, and is furthered by putting oneself in the proper environment for triggering and cultivating that wisdom. "For me," she adds, "it also includes an

Ayurvedic understanding: how to live in harmony with the laws of the living world."

And how does she live the wisdom she carries? "I work with my students and clients to help them see health and life in ways they perhaps hadn't thought of before, and to use practical tools such as herbs, diet, lifestyle modifications, and breath and meditation practices appropriate to their own situation and state of growth. This can bring them to solutions that heal and transform. The seed of the Divine is there within each of us, and with guidance and an environment that nurtures that seed, each of us can become more fully conscious expressions of the Divine."

Sarasvati Buhrman can be reached at 303.443.6923.

Susan Lawrence, M.D.

From the beginning, life felt like a rock in her shoe: uncomfortable, often downright painful, a constant reminder that something didn't quite fit or wasn't quite right. Growing up in Brooklyn, and expected to measure up to the "good Jewish girl" expectations of her family, Susan Lawrence felt as if she was in the wrong time and place, maybe even the wrong body. With memories that seemed to come from an unknown past, an independence unacceptable in her family, and an inner knowing that there was  something for her far beyond what she was living, she found it difficult to feel at home in her own skin. This went beyond the typical angst associated with growing up, and into the realm of those whose gifts are extraordinary.

Accepted at Barnard College at age fourteen, and into medical school at Baylor at seventeen, Susan's academic and intellectual skills were remarkable. Her initial interest in cardiac surgery brought her into contact with exceptional physicians, including Christiaan Barnard, the South African surgeon who had performed the world's first human heart transplant, and Dr. Denton Cooley, another famous heart surgeon at the Texas Heart Institute in Houston. But even with the promise of a brilliant future, Susan found herself in a constant struggle with depression, the source of which she would only discover later, as her work took an unexpected turn.

Choosing medical oncology as her area of specialization, Susan went into private practice working with cancer and AIDS patients. It was during that time that she met and married a deeply insightful and spiritual man who, as a former IV drug user, had contracted the AIDS virus. It was a statement he made that changed Susan's life and work forever. "I'm not dying from AIDS," he said. "I'm dying from the delayed effects of child abuse." This declaration shook Susan's whole world, and changed the way she understood and worked with her patients. "I now realized," she says, "that, although my patients all looked different, under the surface the issues that had contributed to their illnesses were the same. Those underlying root issues had to be addressed for healing to occur." Recognizing the connection between unresolved trauma and illness gave her an entirely new perspective, and her approach to treatment began to shift.

In 1993, Susan founded the Catalyst Foundation, a non-profit organization committed to social change. Their early mission was to provide a wide range of services to those with AIDS. In 1995 they also began to work with adolescents who weren't infected with the AIDS virus, but whose lives were characterized by crime, violence, rage, sorrow, and loneliness, and who, as a result, were engaging in behaviors that negatively impacted their families, communities, and ultimately the whole of society. "I found that it was the same issue, unresolved trauma, that was driving the actions of these kids," she remembers. "Whether it's illness, crime, violence, alcoholism, even war, emotional pain and trauma are the root cause of societal and global problems. When trauma from the past has been healed, the reason for destructive behavior is gone." This applies to depression, too, as Susan found when she did the work necessary to resolve the trauma from her own past. When healing is present, there is no room for depression.

While Susan's staff members continue to work with adolescents, she and Dave Mashore, co-founder of their ground-breaking program, Creating a Healing Society, have begun offering their work in prisons, where they assist incarcerated individuals to change their lives by healing the trauma they have carried. Their prison work began with the help of an extraordinary individual, Ken Hartman, who is serving a life sentence in a California facility, and who had worked to establish an Honor Yard where 600 prisoners chose to devote their lives to peace and positive social change. The Honor Yard has saved the system over $200,000 in its first year alone, has reduced the incidence of violence to almost zero, and has decreased drug use dramatically. Ken began working with Susan and Dave to tailor their program to fit those in prison, and the program they instituted has assisted numerous prisoners in transforming their lives.

"One of the people who participated in our program had barely communicated during his incarceration," Susan recalls. "About half way through our program, he began speaking up and sharing his thoughts and ideas. Everyone was shocked; this was the guy who wouldn't talk. Later, we got a call from a local radio station. They had received a letter from this same man, telling them about our program and how he had grown through participating. His story, and the concepts of the Creating a Healing Society program, were heard by 20,000 people, and that only happened because he had found the courage to work through the trauma that had shaped his life."

The Creating a Healing Society program, as presented in prisons, allows participants, as they near completion of the twelve-week course, to come up with ideas for projects that can be done, either in the prison environment or outside, to promote peace and healing. What Susan Lawrence has found is that, by designing such projects, prisoners begin thinking forward, toward a better kind of life, whether in or out of prison. This serves as yet another motivator offered by the program for healing and transformation. A moving example of the project ideas presented by participants is the one offered by the individual who hadn't communicated before entering the program. His suggestion? Begin a program similar to Toast Masters for prisoners who want to become public speakers.

Susan Lawrence can be reached at www.CreatingAHealingSociety.org.

WOMEN OF POWER

Christy Kopp

For Christy Kopp and her husband Peter, the joy of having a beautiful baby girl quickly turned to anxiety as they noticed an unusual skin condition and the fact that their baby had missed several motor milestones, such as sitting up and crawling. Eventually, little Kayla was diagnosed with Sjogren-Larsson Syndrome, a rare genetic disorder with only about sixty diagnosed cases worldwide. Besides limiting

her motor skills development, the disease causes her skin to constantly grow new cells, making her skin thick, flaky, and painfully itchy.

Dermatologists prescribed harsh chemical treatments for the toddler, but her parents worried about the long-term effects. Christy struggled with the fears and frustration that come with watching your child suffering, and set her mind to finding an answer.

"I've always felt I could shape my own destiny," she explains. "I'm a 'move it forward' kind of person. I had to make a choice; I could feel sorry for myself, or I could gather information and create a plan. That's what I did."

Rather than simply entrusting her child to doctors who had never before seen the condition, Christy began to take action on her own. Through extensive research, much of which presented her with frightening worst case scenarios, she gained enough understanding of the disease to experiment with formulas for moisturizers that could give her baby relief from the itching, and the resulting scratching that often drew blood. "I asked myself 'where are we now, where do we want to be in reference to this situation, and how can we get there?' And then I took action."

Months of arduous research provided Christy with some basic ideas about skin care that might provide Kayla with relief, and she began cooking up a variety of products in her kitchen. "The research was expensive," she remembers. "I was constantly bringing home bags of ingredients from the health food store, and my husband started asking how long I was going to engage in what he was afraid was only a costly hobby. I knew he was concerned about the time and money I was putting into my experimenting, but my daughter's health was at stake; I couldn't stop until I found an answer. I was committed to doing whatever was necessary to give my baby the maximum quality of life."

After using the products recommended by physicians on her own skin and finding that the harsh chemicals burned, Christy decided to no longer even consider using the steroids and petroleum products that had been prescribed for her baby. After more experimenting, she developed her first product: Body Butter. Without any dangerous chemicals, this compound eased Kayla's terrible itching and discomfort, stopped the bleeding caused by scratching, and quickly began healing her earlier lesions. And Elements Home Spa was born.

There were soon additions to her repertoire, and friends began asking her to show the homemade products to groups of their friends. What had begun as a diligent and focused search for a safe way to ease her baby's pain started to snowball. Several home events demonstrated to Christy that she had found something valuable, not only to her own family but also to others. Orders began to pour in, and she knew this was a way to contribute to the quality of life of many beyond her own circle. "I didn't know anything about business," she admits, "but my husband did, and he put together a business plan for me. I told myself that if Kayla is benefiting from what I had come up with, it would be a terrible shame if I didn't make it available to others." In 2002, Christy began selling her products at home events, and in 2003 she started looking for independent sales reps who wanted a way to make money doing something worthwhile that would also allow them more time at home with their families. As of 2006, she has 150 sales consultants who are building financial independence for themselves and their families, thousands of very happy customers all over the U.S., and an eight-year-old Kayla whose health has improved. "She may be in physical therapy for a long time," Christy explains, "and the condition has slowed both her motor and speech development. But she's not in the kind of pain that used to be her everyday reality, because the condition of her skin has improved so much. That's the only result I was going for when I began cooking up skin care recipes in my kitchen." The business has become so successful that the Kopps decided to work as a team, dedicating more resources to the project.

Christy's commitment to quality of life for children has recently expanded her efforts in a new direction. In addition to Elements Home

Spa, she has formed a non-profit organization, Kids Mobility Network, Inc., an entity that provides a resource for families of children with disabilities to attain durable medical equipment. Her goal is to offer an alternative to traditional insurance for under-insured or uninsured families to acquire medical equipment that will provide children with disabilities with greater safety, mobility, and independence.

So, what does this determined and focused woman say to others who want to live powerful and results-filled lives? "Find your passion. It burns from within; when you find it, you'll know."

Christy Kopp can be reached at www.elementshomespa.com

Wangari Maathai

Imagine a land once fertile and forested, but now parched, unsuitable for growing food, and filled with political and mili-

tary conflict. Now imagine that this sorrowful place is where you grew up, your homeland. Imagine the heart-wrenching effect of watching your beloved home shift from lush and welcoming to scorched, hostile, and unsafe. And now consider the courage it would take to make a commitment, in the face of such overwhelming circumstances, to finding a way to help heal the land. This was the experience of an extraordinary woman who is no stranger to powerful and transformational action.

Wangari Maathai, the 2004 winner of the Nobel Peace Prize, is Kenya's Assistant Minister for Environment and Natural Resources, and the founder of the Green Belt Movement. She is a woman of great heart, profound commitment to her homeland, and an unparalleled drive to take action when she sees a pressing need. As a member of the National Council of Women of Kenya in the early 1970s, she listened carefully as rural women spoke of the things they needed and did not have, including clean drinking water, nutritious food, and a safe source of energy. Research taught her that the lack of trees across the country played a huge part in the miserable condition of the homeland she loved. As she further considered the plight of the rural women whose concerns she had heard, a solution took shape in her mind.

"My response was to begin planting trees with them, to help heal the land and break the cycle of poverty. Trees stop soil erosion, leading to water conservation and increased rainfall. As household managers in rural and urban areas of the developing world, women are the first to encounter the effects of ecological stress. It forces them to walk farther to get wood for cooking and heating, to search for clean water and to find new sources of food as old ones disappear."[1]

Her idea grew into the Green Belt Movement, comprised of thousands of groups of mostly women who have planted thirty million trees across Kenya. The women receive payment for each seedling they grow, which provides them with income while improving their environment. Because of its success, the movement has spread to several countries in both East and Central Africa.

Recognizing that corruption and political unrest contributed to the conflicts between factions and the ongoing death of the land, and ensured the continuation of desperate poverty, Wangari knew that planting trees was a powerful first step toward Kenya's healing—but more was required. Human rights violations were happening all over the country; in fact, one of the ways the government retained power was to encourage ethnic groups to attack each other over land. If they stayed busy fighting over land, they would have less time and energy to demand democracy. To help educate and empower the population, Dr. Maathai and her colleagues conducted seminars on human rights, governing, and ways to reduce conflict. Eventually, the Green Belt Movement she had initiated became a leading advocate for fair and free elections in Kenya. Through public education, advocacy, and dangerous public protests, those engaged in the movement worked to protect open spaces and forests from those who sought to develop those areas for personal gain. Because of the stance of the government, harassment, beatings, death threats, and jail time were par for the course for those in the Green Belt Movement, including Dr. Maathai.

In spite of the dangers and demands of her cause, Wangari Maathai remains dedicated to her mission. Her commitment is clear in this statement: "Unless we properly manage resources like forests, water, land, minerals, and oil, we will not win the fight against poverty. And there will not be peace. Old conflicts will rage on and new resource wars will erupt unless we change the path we are on."[2]

Her closing statement as she received the Nobel Peace Prize expressed, in a very few words, the noble character of this exceptional woman: "To celebrate this award, and the work it recognizes of those around the world, let me recall the words of Gandhi: My life is my message. Also, plant a tree."

Dwan Bent-Twyford

At twenty-nine, life was taking shape just as she had learned it should. Married and expecting her first child, Dwan Bent figured she was living the American Dream, or at least parts of it. She planned to be a stay-at-home mom, assumed her marriage would be a forever kind of thing, and felt certain that life would be a comfortable flow. And then everything changed.

One year later, after realizing that she and her husband had very different goals, Dwan was in the middle of a painful and unexpected divorce. This woman who had never held anything but dead end jobs found herself on her own, with an eight-month-old baby to take care of, and $75 to her name. Her first reaction was one of fear and devastation.

"For the first week," she remembers, "all that went through my mind was 'what am I going to do? How can we survive?' For a split second, I thought about moving back home, but I knew that wouldn't work. All I had ever done was low-paying jobs that would take me away from my child and require that I allow strangers to raise my baby. I felt pretty hopeless. After a few days of feeling scared and anxious, I decided it was time to take a clear, hard look at the situation, find the good, the opportunity in it, and make  changes. I had specific goals regarding my child: I wanted her to be ambitious, spiritual, polite, a godly woman, and I wanted to be a good mom. I knew I didn't want to turn her over to a daycare center and take my chances on what kind of person might be passing values and experiences I didn't want for her. The only way to reach my goals for myself and for my child was to turn the situation around and find a way to raise her while working at home. 'I have to make this happen' became the driving slogan in my life, and that's exactly what I did."

Real estate seemed like the most practical choice, but with no money and bad credit, it seemed impossible. But with her baby as her motivation, as well as a strong desire to avoid any "I told you it wouldn't work" feedback from those who thought she was crazy, Dwan borrowed money from relatives and jumped into a world she knew nothing about. Moving quickly from fixing and flipping—learning to do all the work herself!—to real estate wholesaling, Dwan began to realize she had found something that offered financial freedom, plenty of time to be the kind of mother she wanted to be, and an opportunity to help people in need at the same time.

"Besides helping people who were struggling financially and needed to sell their homes fast, it occurred to me that what I was learning to do could provide a new lease on life for others who felt trapped in jobs they hated, and for women who felt trapped in bad, even abusive, relationships because they had become financially dependent on their abusers. I had found a way out for myself and my family, and God laid it on my heart to begin offering to teach other people—especially women who figured they couldn't achieve financial security without a man—to take control of their lives, shape their own destinies, and begin living with the financial freedom and peace of mind I had found."

Another reward has come in the form of a man she met at a conference, and whom she married in 2002. "I used to say that I'd never marry another real estate investor, but then I met Bill Twyford. This man is another of God's gifts to me."

Dwan's commitment to make a difference in the world, her willingness to serve as a conduit for hope and possibility, and her clarity about divine intention and purpose have resulted in an organization, Financial Freedom through Foreclosures, that has taught thousands of individuals how to take the initiative and create freedom, security, and an impressive quality of life for themselves and their families. Comments like "Dwan has changed my life," and "I never thought I could be this successful, and this happy," are common from those who have worked with this woman, who started out waiting tables, and is now a financially independent, sought-after speaker and teacher.

Dwan seems to have time for anyone who truly wants to change the way they live, and she comes across in a down-to-earth and genuine manner, a style that doesn't even hint at the personal and professional success that she's created. There is no arrogance, no pretense about her, as many students have been drawn by her approachability as by the potential available through her work.

Her philosophy is strong and has shaped her life in numerous ways. "I never live in a state of fear," she says. "My parents encouraged me to become whatever I wanted to be, and as a result I find that, even in that difficult time, it never occurred to me that I would fail. I am committed to improving myself, and offering the best service I can to my students and my clients. I tell my students 'You can learn from my experience, but you must find your own motivation. Look deep inside; what motivates you? Focus on that. You can live an amazing life, but you have to make the decision. Search your soul. Find your million dollar motivation.'"

Dwan is a woman for whom humility comes naturally. Rather than taking credit for the ways in which she has helped to change people's lives, she gives credit where she knows it's due. "I used to look around at the people who are unhappy in their jobs, in their relationships, in their lives, and I would say to myself 'If only they could do what I've learned to do, they could change all that.' Now I have a way to make it happen. I have been given something teachable to help others. It's a gift from God."

Dwan Bent-Twyford can be reached at www.1234closures.com.

Jane Mirandette

Until 2000, Nicaragua had no lending libraries. In fact, throughout Central America as a whole there was no access to information for the poor and underprivileged, or for parents wanting information that might help their children improve the quality of their lives. To most people, this fact might seem odd, but easy to dismiss, having no significance in their own lives. To Jane Mirandette, however, it was unacceptable.

At age fifty-six, Jane opened a bed and breakfast in a small coastal town in Nicaragua. To that point, her career had included nursing, public health, and accounting—and it was time for a change. The

venture seemed perfect for both this energetic woman and the man she had been with for several years, and they settled in to their new community, eager to explore a new way of life. To enhance the experience of their guests, Jane provided games and books, in both English and Spanish. She quickly found that, along with a high demand from guests, the books were also being used by her staff and their friends. It was as if they had been starving for information, and had stumbled on a veritable feast. At one point, she suggested that a young girl, thoroughly engaged in a book she had found at the B&B, take it home to finish reading. The idea was unheard of, shocking; and with that Jane's big adventure began.

She started researching, and found that most schools throughout the area had only one or two books per subject for all their students, and that there was virtually no information available in written form. "That lack of information impacts the success of a country," she says. She also found that, although there were libraries in Nicaragua, and throughout Central America, none of them loaned books. Instead, patrons were only allowed to read the books while in the building, and often with a guard nearby to monitor their behavior. Getting access to a catalogue, Jane bought materials for her bed and breakfast and began planning the first lending library in the country. After nine months of preparation, including meetings with officials and educators to ensure approval, the Hotel Villa Isabella lending library opened on the B&B patio.

She quickly had nineteen individuals requesting library cards, and within three months, 400 library patrons were taking advantage of her facility. "We had forty to fifty kids cycling through the place every day," she remembers, "and they came mostly to borrow books, but many came to color. Most of the kids had never colored; teachers in Nicaragua only got one or two pieces of construction paper and one pencil each year. These kids had never had the opportunity to color, and when they learned that I had not only books, but also paper and crayons at the library, they flocked in. It wasn't long before we just couldn't handle the volume on our patio. We needed a building."

In January of 2001, she rented a house around the corner to serve as the library, and things continued to grow. Five years later, the library has 3,500 patrons, over 10,000 books, English classes, space where classes on a variety of subjects can be offered to the community, and craft classes. Students use the space to do their homework, and it's become a kind of community center for the area.

Recently, and in great part as a result of Jane's efforts, there is a much greater emphasis on literacy in Nicaragua. A Spanish version of the "At Your Library" campaign publicizing programs offered at local libraries—which has been in place in the US for years—is now in full swing in this Central American country. Called "En Tu Biblioteca," the campaign informs the community of the programs and services available at their libraries. The tight control and limited access that had characterized all facets of education have begun to shift, and people of all ages are learning and growing in ways they had never imagined.

What moved this unpretentious woman to take action that has affected the direction of an entire country? "I believe I can make a difference in the world," she states simply. "I am always looking for the next way I can be of service. I believe that women, especially middle-aged women, can feel invisible and insignificant; but I refuse to be swallowed up by people who think middle-aged women are irrelevant, or by circumstances that seem overwhelming. There are things that need to be done in the world, and I can help."

A clear indication of the character of this powerful yet down-to-earth woman lies in a decision she made during a painful time. The library was growing and had begun to play an important part in the life of the community, when Jane experienced a couple of personal losses that threw her into a cycle of grief almost too much to bear. "I remember thinking 'I have to leave; this is too painful.'" But, as she considered packing up and leaving Nicaragua, she realized it wasn't an option. "What will happen to my library if I'm gone?" she worried, and that concern shaped her decision to remain, despite the personal pain. "I had a choice: I could abandon all we had created, run away, and experience even more loss (by giving up the library), or I could stick it out, deal with the loss, and move on."

Jane is the Founder and Director of the San Juan del Sur Biblioteca Publica Y Movil, Nicaragua's first lending library and mobile library project, and she has helped facilitate the creation of nine other library lending and community center projects. Three more libraries guided by Jane and under the direction of Wisconsin Nicaragua Partners of the Americans (WNPA) will open this year. She is a member of the American Library Association (ALA), the International Relations Round Table (IRRT), International Federation of Library Associations (IFLA), and most recently, the Nicaraguan Library Association (ANIBIPA). She is also President of the Hester J. Hodgdon Libraries for All program. Her most important credentials for starting and running public libraries lies in the fat that she is not afraid of steep learning curves, and has learned through her three grandchildren to appreciate what abundant access to books can do for children.

What guidance does this determined and tireless woman offer to women who want to find deeper meaning in their lives? "Read all you can by and about evolved women. Find that resonant place in yourself, and allow yourself the privilege of finding your own power."

In November 2005, Jane's library celebrated its fourth anniversary. A poetry contest was held to select the best poem to express what the facility and its services meant to the community. The following is the winning work, written by a fourteen-year-old Nicaraguan girl, whose heartfelt appreciation was echoed by the entire community:

Happy Birthday Biblioteca Movil

With balloons of colors
Ribbons and streamers
There is festivity in our hearts
On this 4th anniversary of our library.

From her there is joy
and to us a better future
For this we celebrate on this day
With soul, life and heart.

Coming to us are one thousand books
to read with our attention
And coming to her, 100,000 niños
To celebrate this day with love.

Library, from you I have the total of my wisdom
and so this poem is for you
and because you have illuminated my days
Today I give you my gratitude.

First Place Winner
Rhina Ercilia Guadalupe Pomares Herrera, Age 14

Feliz Cumpleaños Biblioteca Movil

Con globos de colores,

Listones y paletas

Se festeja en nuestros corazones

el 4to aniversario de nuestra biblioteca.

De ella es la alegria

y de nosotros un futuro mejor

por esa celebremos en este día

Con alma, vida y corazón.

Vengan a nosotros mil libros

para leer con atención

y vengan a ella 100,000 niños

para celebra este día con amor.

Ya que eres toda mi sabiduría

entonces este poema es para ti

y porque has iluminado mis días

hoy te doy las gracias así.

Primer Lugar
Rhina Ercilia Guadalupe Pomares Herrera, 14 Años

Jane Mirandette can be reached at www.sjdsbiblioteca.com.

WOMEN OF THE SENSES

Bette Midler

An icon of the American theater, film, and music scenes, Bette Midler expresses with elegance and vibrancy what life can be when it's well informed by the senses. Her *joie de vivre* is contagious, her performances vivacious, and her unmistakable energy draws audiences into her world, even if only briefly, and demonstrates just how much passion and beauty life can hold.

Born in Honolulu in 1945, her interest in the performing arts began in childhood, and has continued, un-waver-ing, for half a century through a dynamic parade of both personal and professional triumphs and tragedies. With both numerous successes and a number of unsuccessful ventures under her belt, her performances continue to be tributes to the passion and delight available through the sensual nature.

Her ability to read an audience, sense its collective mood, and shape her performances accordingly depends, in great part, on her sensory acuity, her skill in receiving information provided by the senses, and applying that information effectively. That skill, and her immense talent as an actor, dancer, and vocalist have ensured for her the highest level of respect from the entertainment community—from Hollywood to Broadway, and everywhere between. Her gift for tapping into what her senses are telling her and responding appropriately has allowed her to develop and refine a broad range in her work: Her successes reach from gay clubs to musical theater to films depicting despair. This is a remarkable woman.

It is probably true of all great performers, whatever their genre, that awareness of the senses plays an essential part in their success. Success in any field requires that all the relevant information available be implemented, and in a field in which the immediate response of others either deflates or energizes the performer, knowing how to tap into and apply sensory data becomes crucial.

On stage, in film, and in her albums, Bette fairly bursts with an energy that implies she's in on something the rest of us have missed. Although she presents herself with obvious sensuality, there is a kind of excitement about her that's almost childlike, as if she finds life so thrilling, so stimulating, that she can barely contain the exuberance. The excitement she carries seems to suggest to the rest of us that there's more to experience, more passion, more beauty, more joy than we may realize.

Bette Midler, whose backup singers were at one time called the Harlettes, is an excellent example of this archetype who lives life fully open and fully aware.

Holly Marsland

When Holly Marsland enters a room, everything changes. The energy she carries ramps it all up a notch or two, and suddenly things look brighter, more intriguing, and as if there's every reason to regard life with a playful eye. Combine that with her spiritual depth, and you've got a woman to contend with.

Holly is a Reiki master; she's practiced the ancient energetic therapy, known to bring physical, emotional, and spiritual bodies into greater balance, since 1997, attaining the level of master in 2002. Her earlier career, graphic design, allowed her to use and refine her creativity and her skill in visualizing graphic solutions to her clients' needs. Although the work helped her connect with people to some degree, she was eager to find a way to shape connections at a deeper level, and to help people in a life-changing way.

Reiki has been practiced for 2,500 years, and theories of its origin range from Japan, to Tibet ... to Atlantis. Needless to say, moving from the familiar and well-accepted world of graphic design to the practice of an art ancient enough that its origin is uncertain, and far removed from mainstream ideas about both therapy and spirituality, required a big dose of both courage and trust. But Holly rose to the occasion immediately. "Reiki came to me so naturally," she says. "No complications, no struggle, very  few questions; I simply knew it was where I belonged. It felt so right, like slipping in through an open doorway."

Born and raised in South Africa, Holly was diagnosed, at the tender age of sixteen months, with a retinal blastoma, a cancerous tumor on the optic nerve. She experienced the maximum chemotherapy and radiation deemed safe for such a young child, but eventually the decision was made to prevent the spread of the cancer and save her life by doing surgery. Her right eye was removed immediately, leaving only the socket. This began a life that many might have regarded as limited, but not Holly. "As a result of losing my eye, my other senses have been honed and intensified," she assures me. "I have always been so aware of the information I get through my senses, and I believe that, in part, that awareness has developed as compensation for the loss of my eye."

Reiki has also contributed to her sensory acuity and, in turn, being more aware of her senses has allowed her to become a more effective practitioner. "I can feel what's going on with my clients, and sense the deeper issues to address. That helps me stay in tune with them as we work together. As I grow through the work I do, my work with clients happens at a more profound level. Reiki encourages me to go deeper into the discovery of my own essence. It brings to life everything at the core of me, and ignites what is innate in me. Physically, it helps maintain balance, and helps my senses stay open and receptive. And as I work with my clients, I find that Reiki awakens parts of the self that can help them become everything they want to be. Reiki leads to an open heart, non-judgment, and many possibilities for healing."

Holly lights up when her sensual nature and her sensory awareness are the topic of conversation. "I am so aware of my senses that life feels like a big box of gifts to open each day. It can be exhausting, if I let it, because there's so much coming at me all the time. Occasionally, I have to turn it off so it isn't overwhelming." Even as she is aware of the possible overwhelm, she understands that her senses put her in touch with what's right for her, and assist her to make choices and decisions that work in both her career and her personal life.

And what is everyday life like for a woman so in touch with her sensual nature? "I have always lived for the experience and joy that can be found everywhere, and my experiences are based on and led by my senses. I love being able to do what feels good to me without hurting anyone."

Two elements that allow her to express her sensual nature in appropriate ways, enhancing her own life and the lives of those around her in the process, are elegance and authenticity. "As long as I am being authentic and expressing myself in a tasteful and elegant way, pretty much anything I say or do works well. There is great freedom in that. When I remember that I am perfect exactly as I am in the moment, the power in me is awakened."

Holly's femininity is part of her charm, but don't mistake femininity for submissiveness. "I'm real, and I have a soft side, but I'm not timid; I have strong opinions, and I don't hesitate to express them when it's useful. " Her understanding of justice, honesty, respect, and kindness make her a powerful and profound spiritual teacher and a delightful role model for those who want to be sensual, feminine, and powerful simultaneously. And with all humility, she understands herself to be a conduit, awakening that which is already in each person with whom she comes in contact.

Her suggestion for anyone wanting to become more aware of their senses is simple: "Take notice of the smallest things, and don't take them for granted. Also, listen more than you speak. In the process you will engage all your senses."

How does she describe life lived with senses wide open? "Have you ever been high without using any drugs? That's what life can be."

Holly Marsland can be reached at www.reikiwithholly.com.

June Craven

June Craven has become a high altitude kind of gal. This small, almost delicate looking woman has climbed all fifty-four mountains in Colorado of 14,000 feet in altitude or higher, and several even higher peaks in the Everest region in Nepal. What she has found in the process is that spending time in sync with nature enriches her on many levels, strengthens her, and reminds her of everything she is capable of.

June's love of mountain climbing began almost by accident when, in 1989, friends invited her to join them in climbing Long's Peak, a popular climber's destination in Colorado. Her friends' goal was to take sunrise photos from the summit, and the visual impact from that vantage point dazzled her. From that moment, she was hooked. The richness of the experience, the visual beauty, the sounds and smells found only in a natural and uncluttered environment shifted her focus from the distractions of everyday life to something much deeper, much more rewarding. "It felt like coming home," she recalls. Eager to have more of this profound sensory experience, she made a commitment to explore the Colorado mountains. She climbed all fifty-four Colorado peaks in five summers, completing twenty-seven in one summer—twenty of them by herself. Because many technical climbers train in Colorado as they prepare to take on the world's most intimidating peaks, June was able to learn more by forming bonds, however brief, with serious climbers she met on the trail. As her interest increased, she took a climbing class at a local free university where the instructor spoke about the experiences she had climbing in Nepal. As June listened, she was fascinated with the possibilities. "If she can do it, so can I," she thought; and thus began a whole new adventure.

In 1999, she traveled to the Everest region in Nepal, hired a porter, and began exploring both the extraordinary area and her own courage and skill. Her experience climbing in Nepal was so remarkable that she's gone back twice, climbing several peaks over 18,000 feet. On her second trip, June went as a guide to a seventy-five-year-old woman, Harriett, who wanted to climb a peak parallel to Everest, at an altitude of 18,300 feet. Her goal was to do it as a memorial to both her son, who had been killed in a climbing accident, and her husband who, although he was wheelchair-bound with multiple sclerosis, motivated her to get involved in cycling and to ride more than 100,000 miles over a brief period of time. June hired two sherpanas (female sherpas), and the four of them spent twenty-six days in the region, ultimately reaching the summit, where Harriett created the memorial that was so meaningful to her.

Why has she chosen this kind of physical challenge as a source of satisfaction in her life? "I have a learning disability, and because of that a lot of things have been difficult for me. But climbing came so naturally; this was something I could do and feel good about. The effect on my senses, spending time in beautiful natural setting, is huge. I find joy in those places, and I am reminded of how much beauty there is in the world. Any problems I'm dealing with just seem to melt away when I'm climbing and feeling in harmony with nature. I can capture some of that beauty—the mountain, flowers, trees, and animals—in the photographs I take while I'm there, and those serve to keep me focused on that beauty and harmony even when life seems difficult. I find myself in a state of awe and wonder in these stunning places, and that helps me remember to look for things of awe and wonder in the other parts of my life."

Climbing has also helped her stay aware of how fortunate and how strong she is. "I can go anywhere and see amazing things. I am healthy and strong, and I am not limited physically. I feel so lucky to be able to have these experiences. I have also learned through climbing just how much I can handle in other areas of my life. When things seem tough, personally or professionally, I remind myself that if I can handle 18,000-foot peaks, I can handle just about anything."

As a woman who lives in a sensory-rich inner and outer world, June knows that climbing is a source of profound reward for her. "It reminds me that there is incredible beauty in the world. When I am on the top of a mountain and enjoying an amazing view, I remember how unlimited opportunities are in life. I can smell the rich fragrance of cedar and other woods, and appreciate the absence of city fumes; and the sounds of birds singing in an environment that is natural to them add to the wonderful feelings I have when I climb. I also love the feeling of community I get when I meet other climbers on the trail. Even if we simply say 'hello' and move on, I know we have something deep in common, a profound love of nature and everything it provides."

June offers easy-to-follow guidance for women who want that same sensory richness: "Make a decision, a commitment to yourself, to find something that will enrich you, and offer you joy. Read about it; research it so you know how to get started. Then just jump in and do it. You'll look back later and realize how much richer your life has become."

June Craven can be reached at bjune55@msn.com.

Grandma Moses

Born Anna Mary Robertson on September 7, 1860, and married to Thomas Salmon Moses in 1887, America's most renowned and best-loved primitive-style folk artist spent most of her life as a farmer's wife and the mother of five children. Until late in her life, her favorite

pastime was embroidery, which she abandoned in her seventies because arthritis had made such intricate work impossible.

It was after giving up embroidery, in her mid-seventies, that Anna Mary Robertson began painting. With no training and no experience, this genuine, down-to-earth farmer's wife simply decided to find a new way to express her-

self—and the result was a style that appealed to almost everyone, from educated art critics to housewives and farmhands. The epitaph on her gravestone at the Maple Grove Cemetery in New York explains the power of her work: "Her primitive paintings captured the spirit and preserved the scene of a vanishing countryside."

Her work was first noticed in 1938 when she was seventy-eight. An art collector noticed her paintings in a drugstore window, and purchased them. These were the first pieces to sell in a long parade of artistic triumphs she would enjoy throughout the rest of her life. One year later, Otto Kallir, an art dealer in New York City, exhibited her work at his Gallerie Saint-Etienne, in a one-woman show that brought her national recognition. That show thrust her into the art world limelight, and collectors and dealers all over the world soon sought after her paintings. There were numerous exhibitions of her work in Europe and as far away as Japan, where her paintings were particularly well received. In 1949, President Harry S. Truman presented her with the Women's National Press Club Award for outstanding accomplishment in art.

Her style was simple, and her themes mostly rural. As her work progressed through more than twenty prolific years, it was obvious that she was recapturing images, sounds, feelings, tastes, and smells of a lifestyle that was rapidly disappearing—a lifestyle that had shaped her own experience. The sensory information presented in her work brings with it feelings of peace, security, community, and a simpler time.

At the age of 100, she illustrated *The Night Before Christmas* by Clement Moore, a book published after her death. Grandma Moses died on December 13, 1961 at age 101. During the last year of her life, she created twenty-five new paintings.

All these individuals, whether famous or not, are demonstrations of what is possible when a woman chooses to live her life from a place of profound power, wisdom, and sensuality. Whether actor, housewife, farmer, poet, or grandmother, the spark of the Divine lies within, always available, just waiting for the invitation to emerge and shape life to its grandest form. This is true for each of us; when you are living the life of The Bitch, The Crone, and The Harlot you move others to seek their own highest and best, no matter who you are.

Bibliography

1. Almaas, A.H. *Diamond Heart—Book One.* Berkeley: Almaas Publications, 1987.

2. Arrien, Angeles. *The Four-Fold Way.* Harper San Francisco, 1993.

3. Bolen, Jean. *The Tao of Psychology.* Harper San Francisco, 1979.

4. Brehony, Kathleen. *Awakening At Midlife.* New York: Riverhead Books, 1996.

5. Bristol, Claude. *The Magic of Believing.* Englewood Cliffs: Prentice-Hall, 1948.

6. Chopra, Deepak. *Ageless Body, Timeless Mind.* New York. Three Rivers Press, 1993.

7. Choquette, Sonia. *Your Heart's Desire.* New York: Three Rivers Press, 1997.

8. Chu, Chin-Ning. *Do Less, Achieve More.* New York: ReganBooks, 1998.

9. Edinger, Edward. *Ego and Archetype.* New York: Penguin Books, 1972.

10. Hanh, Thich Nhat. *The Miracle of Mindfulness.* Boston: Beacon Press, 1975.

11. Hendricks, Gay & Ludeman, Kate. *The Corporate Mystic.* New York: Bantam Books, 1996.

12. Hicks, Esther and Jerry. *Ask and It Is Given.* Carlsbad: Hay House, 2004.

13. Hyde, Laura. *Gifts of the Soul.* Sustainable Solutions Press, 1997.

14. Johnson, Robert. *Inner Work.* San Francisco: Harper & Row, 1986.

15. Ladinsky, Daniel (translator). *The Gift-Poems of Hafiz.* New York, Penguin/Arkana, 1999.

16. Northrup, Christiane, M.D. *Women's Bodies, Women's Wisdom.* Westminster, Maryland: Bantam Dell Publishing Group, 19 98.

17. O'Connor, Joseph & Seymour, John. *Introducing NLP.* San Francisco: Thorsons, 1990.

18. Peirce, Penney. *The Intuitive Way.* Hillsboro: Beyond Words Publishing, 1997.

19. Sargent, Allen. *The Other Mind's Eye.* Malibu: Success Design International Publications, 1999.

Endnotes

The Bitch

[1] Proverbs 23:7, KJV .

[2] *Hamlet,* Act II, Scene II, William Shakespeare (1601).

The Crone

[1] Brehony, Kathleen A. *Awakening At Midlife.* Riverhead Books, 1996, p. 142.

[2] *ibid.,* p. 18.

[3] Lama Yeshe and Lama Zopa Rinpoche. *Wisdom Energy.* Wisdom Publications, Australia, 2000.

[4] Gautama Buddha (Richards, John, tr). *The Dhammapada.* Ancient World Cultures Online. Reprinted from http://eawc.evansville.edu/anthology/dhammapada.htm.

[5] Lao Tzu (McDonald, J.H., tr.). *Tao Te Ching.* Reprinted from www.wam.umd.edu/-stwright/rel/tao/TaoTeChing.html.

[6] *The Quiet Mind, Sayings of White Eagle,* The White Eagle Publishing Trust, Hampshire, England, 1972, p. 30.

The Harlot

[1] *Bad Case of Loving You,* written by John Martin, performed by Robert Palmer (1979).

[2] UC Irvine researchers have found that men and women have very different brain designs. Women have more much white matter and men more gray matter related to intelligence. Still, there are no real differences in general intelligence between the two sexes. From the UCI press release about the study:

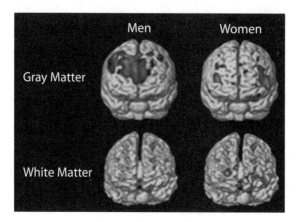

Gray matter represents information processing centers in the brain, and white matter represents the networking of—or connections between—these processing centers.

This, according to Rex Jung, a UNM neuropsychologist and co-author of the study, may help to explain why men tend to excel in tasks requiring more local processing (like mathematics), while women tend to excel at integrating and assimilating information from distributed gray-matter regions in the brain, such as is required for language facility. These two very different neurological pathways and activity centers, however, result in equivalent overall performance on broad measures of cognitive ability, such as those found on intelligence tests.

Getting There
[1] Matthew 12:45, KJV .

Bringing Your Gifts to the World
[1] Kluger, Jeffrey. *Time Magazine.* January 16, 2006.

Honoring (and Becoming) the Archetypes
[1] "Trees for Democracy: Wangari Maathai." *New York Times,* December 10, 2004.
[2] *ibid.*